Children Together

Volume 3

A PROGRAM RESOURCE FOR BOYS AND GIRLS • GRADES 3-6

Gracie Rose McCay and Virginia A. Sargent, editors

Illustrated by Joni Fredman

Judson Press ® Valley Forge

CHILDREN TOGETHER, VOLUME 3

Copyright © 1985
Judson Press, Valley Forge, PA 19482-0851

ISBN 0-8170-1078-5
The name JUDSON PRESS is registered as a trademark in the U.S. Patent Office.
Printed in the U.S.A. ⊕

Photo credits: Pages 7, 9, 23, 53, 86, Camerique; 27, 61, 67, Strix Pix; 37, Vivienne; 44, Paul M. Schrock; 51, Alan Cliburn; 57, Jean-Claude Lejeune; 71, 76, American Baptist Churches, U.S.A., Board of International Ministries and Board of National Ministries; 82, UNICEF; 97, 107, 110, 112, 113, American Baptist Historical Society; 114, Three Lions.

Contents

Introduction

What It Is

Children Together, Volume 3 is a program resource. It is a smorgasbord of ideas and plans from which you can pick and choose.

The units are not arranged in a particular order and are not dated. They may be used in any order and at any time when they are most appropriate in your situation.

Six of the eight units contain four sessions. The other two each contain five sessions. Some of the units have more than enough material so that the leader may add an extra session. Note that the sessions in *Children Together, Volume 3* are planned for 60 minutes. If you have less time than one hour, you may use the plans of one session for two sessions. Or you may choose to do only a portion of the activities.

When to Use It

Like its predecessors, *Children Together, Volume 3* is a program resource for use with children in grades three through six in settings other than church school. Churches have found many different times and ways to use *Children Together:*

- on Sunday or weekday evenings
- for weekday after-school groups
- for a weekend retreat for children
- for intergenerational events
- on Sunday mornings during adult worship
- for boys' groups and for girls' groups

Occasionally a unit from *Children Together* may be substituted for a unit in the regular church school curriculum. *Children Together* is a resource which can be used at almost any time children meet with caring adults.

How to Use It

Look through the whole book. Get acquainted with it. Discover the subjects of the units. If you plan to use it over an extended period with the same group, make a tentative plan of the order in which you will use the eight units. If you are looking for resources for a particular event, such as a weekend retreat, look through the material with that in mind.

When you have decided on a unit, read it through carefully. Note any resources which you will need to order and send for them well in advance. Make a list of all the suggested activities. Are all of them possible in your situation? If not, what can you substitute? Are there any activities with which you will need more help? What special materials do you need to assemble?

Now make a step-by-step plan for each session of the unit. Do the necessary preparation, gather the materials, try all activities, and arrange for any special resource people or additional help.

Most sessions call for the use of chalkboard and/or newsprint. Newsprint is unprinted newspaper which is available in large sheets or in rolls. Any large sheets of paper with one blank side may be used when newsprint is suggested. The advantage of using paper instead of, or in addition to, a chalkboard is that it can be posted, saved, and added to throughout the unit.

Frequently it is suggested that children be invited to participate in a time of prayer, to share something they have made or written, or to respond to a question. While it is important to encourage this kind of participation, it is even more important that children who are not ready to share may have the right to turn down the opportunity without being made to feel guilty or embarrassed.

Music can be an important part of sessions with children. If you are uncomfortable in this area, try to find someone who can assist with the music. There may be a child in the group who could learn and teach songs, or there may be a parent, a youth, or an adult who would be happy to help in this way. If your group meets at a time when it is difficult for other people to participate, you could ask someone to record the songs on tape to help you learn the songs and/or to use them with the children.

Stories are often the heart of the session. They are used for a variety of reasons—to give information, to summarize, to challenge, to inspire, or to present a problem to be solved.

Whether stories are told or read, they must be well done! Let's look at some ways to be an effective story-teller or reader.

- Read the story aloud.
- Determine the story's purpose in the session.
- Decide whether you will tell or read the story.
- Read it aloud again, noting the progression of the action.
- Make an outline of the story. If you plan to tell it, jot down on a card a few key words or phrases—the

opening, the main events, the climax.

- Practice telling or reading the story. Use direct discourse when appropriate. Try to make the story come alive for yourself and for those who will hear it.

When the session is over, take a few minutes to evaluate. What went particularly well? Why? What would you do differently another time? How do you feel about the session? You may want to make some notes in the book at the end of the session.

The Children with Whom It Is Used

It is impossible to describe a typical child of any age because there is no such thing as a typical child. We can, however, note some rather common characteristics of children of the same age, while at the same time we keep aware of the broad range of individual differences.

Third graders are usually active, speedy, and aware persons who like to discover new things and for whom relationships with others are very important.

Fourth graders are also active and tend to be more confident and independent but may be withdrawn at times. They like to do things with adults and are often perfectionists.

Fifth and sixth graders are busy, noisy, competitive, and curious. Their friendships tend to be with others of the same sex because girls are often ahead of boys in their physical and social development.

What happens when children of all these ages are together in one group? Some guidelines for dealing with such a group follow.

- Relate to the children as individuals, recognizing the talents, abilities, and limitations of each. Sixth graders may be better readers than most third graders, but it is quite likely that some third graders will have developed some skills, such as in art or music, beyond those of some sixth graders.
- Encourage children to work together to accomplish the task at hand. Learning is most apt to take place in an atmosphere of cooperation, rather than competition, in which each child is valued for his or her own unique place in the group.
- Encourage children to ask one another for help. Emphasize that asking for help is a sign of strength, not of weakness.
- Provide opportunities for children to form subgroups according to their interests rather than on the basis of age.
- Think of yourself as a learner as well as a teacher. Be open to what you can learn with and from the children.

It's Time to Begin

Your plans are made, materials are ready, and you are well prepared. Offer yourself as a channel of God's love to the boys and girls who will look to you as their leader.

And be expectant! Anticipate being with children together with JOY. It will be catching!

Who Wrote It?

Each unit of *Children Together, Volume 3* was written by a different person. These persons were asked to write because of their particular knowledge, skills, and experience in related areas.

"Jesus in the Electronic Age" was written by Daniel Holland. Dan lives in Springfield, Illinois, and is an area minister for American Baptist Churches of the Great Rivers Region. He also serves as Director of Media Services for that region. He has written, edited, and produced numerous electronic resources.

"The Things That Make for Peace" was written by Betty Grant. Betty lives in Ridgewood, New Jersey, and, in addition to writing, has served as a leader in leader training events nationally and regionally. She is director of a child day care center in Ridgewood, New Jersey.

"Learning About the Bible" was written by Phyllis Heusser. Phyllis lives in Boise, Idaho, and is a curriculum writer and counselor. She has been a leader in leader training events both regionally and nationally.

"Children Face Life's Crises" was written by Marie Anderson. Marie lives in Charleston, Illinois. She is a curriculum writer and has written video scripts. She is involved in leader training.

"Partners in Mission" was written by Arline Ban. Arline lives in Ontario, Canada. She is the author of numerous books, articles, and curriculum. She is a Christian educator and workshop leader.

"Sharing, Saving, Spending" was written by Joy Ng. Joy is an artist, writer, and musician and is actively involved in her church in Exton, Pennsylvania. She lives in Malvern, Pennsylvania.

"The Chapel Car Ministry" was written by Eula Fresch, of King of Prussia, Pennsylvania. Eula is a curriculum writer, Christian educator, and a public school and church school teacher.

"Saints of God" was written by Steve Edwards. Steve lives in Prairie Village, Kansas, and is Director of Christian Education at Prairie Baptist Church. He is a writer involved in leader training both regionally and nationally. He is also active in clown ministry.

UNIT 1

Jesus in the Electronic Age

by Daniel W. Holland

Unit Introduction

Fire, the plow, electricity, the automobile, computers! Think of the number of people who, over thousands of years, have shaken their heads and muttered that they prefer the old ways instead of these newfangled ideas and gadgets. When we don't understand something, we naturally long for the "good old days."

The focus of this unit is to explore the importance of human relationships; because we also live in a world that is experiencing the "Information Revolution." As a teacher, you might find that your students are ahead of you in being familiar with the rapidly growing world of electronic technology. In contrast you may be much more sensitive to the biblical mandate to care about people and keep the value of

"things" in true perspective. This difference can provide an excellent background for a delightful time of learning together and from each other.

As you prepare for this unit, you may want to examine your theology a bit. Do you agree with the Psalmist that "the cattle on a thousand hills" are God's (Psalm 50:10) and with the hymn writer that "all good things around us are sent from heaven above"? Does this apply to all those complex, sophisticated games and computers that are capturing so much attention these days? The computer equipment called hardware is certainly different from anything known to people of an earlier day, but the decisions involved in the use of equipment like this are those that have been faced by every human since time began. These have to do with the question: "How will I best use God's good gifts to me?'' One of God's best gifts to humankind is creative intelligence. How will I use the fruits of that gift? Will I find my meaning in life in these things? Will I value them above persons? Will I use these creations for the good of others or to destroy?

There's no lack of biblical material for our instruction when it comes to this topic of keeping the balance between technical equipment and the value of persons. Jesus' life was one of keeping things and people in proper perspective. One of your best challenges as a teacher is to help children appreciate the universality and also the uniqueness of the decisions that they face. The Sermon on the Mount said much about where real value is to be found. The story of the Rich Young Ruler deals with hard choices (see Matthew 19:16-30). Even the ancient, mythical King Midas story is a nonbiblical lesson about these values. The uniqueness of the world into which your class members are growing is due to its rapid change and the ways in which ''things'' are replacing direct personal relationships. The Rich Young Ruler had to deal with servants, camel salesmen and a host of others! Your learners, on the other hand, are growing into a world which will allow them to become much more remote from other people, if they so choose.

You may have become aware of the increasing number of articles that are appearing in newspapers and magazines expressing concern about the computer in particular. Not all of these articles are by reactionaries who want to return to the mythical ''good old days,'' by any means. Even those people who are exploring ways to use the computer in education are cautioning that there can be a loss of social skills involved in its use, and the assumption that the computer will become the salvation of education is not to be trusted.

An interesting sidelight to the labor-saving value of computers and other technological breakthroughs is that, as persons are able to work at home from remote terminals, they may become a new kind of ''workaholic.'' One may get to the point where she or he never leaves the workplace, since the terminal and the telephone are always nearby!

The issues we will be exploring in this unit will be those of proper use of computers and other technological machines. Perhaps you are coming to this study with some biases of your own. You might be a computer ''widow'' or ''widower,'' or you might be having difficulty keeping the channels of communication open with a member of your own family who spends too much time and money on electronic games. Work very hard to avoid defining the Christian faith as something that should be opposed to modern technology. Persons in your group need to discover how to live and minister in these rapidly changing and technologically sophisticated days.

Read through the sessions and notice that it is suggested that you use some equipment that is not normally a part of your classroom. This will take some extra effort and advance planning, but it is important that this be a ''doing'' and not just a ''talking'' time together with your group.

One way to experience the connection between the Bible and our computer age is to use the game which has been included at the end of this book. As the instructions indicate, it has been designed for use in several brands of computers which use BASIC as their language. Perhaps one or two of the children in your group would be willing to put the game onto their machines, instead of your doing it yourself. This would have the definite advantage of using the abilities of learners and generating interest.

You will need to plan to have the game put into the computer before, rather than during, the session in which you plan to use it. Loading the game may take one-half to one hour depending on the speed and accuracy of the typist.

Make the effort to have the games and computer available so that you can enjoy technology together as you talk about its proper use. Show yourself to be a willing pupil as you learn from your class about the ''latest and best!''

Here are some suggestions for the preparation of your room. Instead of using ordinary mimeo paper for writing assignments, why not use regular computer printer paper with the punched edges? Many department stores are now carrying small packets of this paper in their home-computer departments. Ask someone involved in data processing for some used fanfold sheets full of indecipherable numbers that you can drape from your bulletin board. Find pictures of microwave dishes, computers, calculators, TVs, satellites, games, etc. Ask a willing group member to draw a satellite system on the chalkboard.

One of the purposes of this unit is also to learn to appreciate the place of traditional arts, crafts, and hobbies. Think about the unique gifts that God has given to each one in your group and be prepared to draw attention to these at an appropriate time. The third session will suggest particular ways to explore the values of these nonelectronic facets of life. Begin to think about others in your church who might be invited to share with your group.

The last session (on violence), while not directly computer related, is appropriate because of the continuing questioning of the impact of violence seen on television and in electronic games. A high percentage of the arcade and home games are built around the challenge of ''blasting'' an enemy. What is the effect of this kind of play on young people? Is it negative or simply neutral?

Several carefully documented studies have been done on the impact of antisocial television scenes on an audience. The more subtle result of lessening persons' sensitivity to one another is one that concerns Christian parents and teachers. Someone has said that the opposite of love is not hate but *not caring*. These sessions will be an opportunity to explore together with your class the true nature of *caring* as modeled by Jesus.

Materials to Have Ready

It is helpful to have available newsprint and markers, crayons, scissors, pencils, paper, and Bibles. In addition to items already mentioned, you may want to gather the following materials:

Session 1: ● electronic or computer games
   ● computers borrowed from church members or possibly dealers

Session 2: ● number badges made of construction paper and string

Session 3: ● paper prepared as time charts

Session 4: ● electronic or computer games as in Session 1

Resources for This Unit

Books

Millgram, S., and Shotland, L., *Television and Anti-Social Behavior: Field Experiments*. New York: Academic Press, 1973.

Films

All films listed are available from Mass Media Ministries, 2116 North Charles Street, Baltimore, MD 21218. Phone (301) 727-3270.

TV—The Anonymous Teacher—Color, 15 minutes, $20.00 rental.

A brief, high-impact treatment of a current social problem. Interviews with psychologists on the effects of TV are punctuated with film clips of young children watching television.

Kids for Sale—Color, 22 minutes, $30.00 rental.

Documents the commercial exploitation of children by television broadcasters and advertisers. This hard-hitting documentary, produced by Action for Children's Television, graphically illustrates how commercial television shapes the outlook, insights, and values of our nation's children.

The 30-Second Dream—Color, 15 minutes, $25.00 rental.

Effectively demonstrates how creators of commercials play on our hopes and fears for essential areas of concern to all Americans: Family, Intimacy, Vitality, and Success. An excellent resource.

Television—The Enchanted Mirror—Color, 28 minutes, $35.00 rental.

Offers an eye-opening look at some of the issues raised by the medium which, as one TV critic and writer claims, "wants to keep you asleep." For senior highs and adults. The leaders may wish to view it before teaching the unit.

Session 1

The World of Electronics

Purpose

- To look at and participate consciously in the world of electronics.
- To discover and list the values that electronics offers for our lives.
- To appreciate modern technology as a part of God's good gifts to us.

Background for Leader(s)

When children play hide and seek, they often say, "Ready or not, here I come!" That cry would be appropriate for all of us as we begin this unit on the Electronic Age. Adults may not be ready for the changes that are happening all too rapidly for comfort. Children, on the other hand, do not have this sense of uneasiness and accept these startling discoveries and rapid-paced developments as normal to their lives.

Remember that the children in your group have never known a world without color television or inexpensive calculators. The youngest ones grew up with video games. The schools they attend very likely have several computers and may be offering computer classes to kindergarteners. These children accept as normal a channel-hopping interaction with the TV that takes them from cartoons to live news of warfare to exciting dramas with gadgets galore. The press of a button can do marvelous things. And with the use of video recorders children can see the most exciting parts over and over. This is one arena where a person can feel in charge of his or her world; press a button, move a joystick, aim the remote control, and the electronic servants quietly obey.

This session is an introduction to a four-session look at this wonderful world of electronics, with particular concern for "people values" which might easily be roughly pushed aside or, more typically, gradually ignored. As you noticed in the suggested purposes, however, the session will be a time of participating in this world.

Did you read the unit introduction? Did you take time to examine your own views of how television, video games, and computers could possibly be understood as some of God's good gifts to the world? (This may be very difficult for adults who have lost patience with local game parlors!) A part of this session will be used to give thanks to God for the good gifts of technology and intelligence while beginning to become aware of the difficult choices that confront humankind in this technological world.

This should be a "doing" session, and you will need to make careful advance preparations. Resist the temptation simply to assume that the suggested equipment is not available in your church family! Members of your class can make suggestions and help you gather things together.

Advance Preparations

You will need to arrange for a variety of video games and, if possible, a home computer.

Consider using the game "Bible Knowledge," found on pages 19-22 of this book, or other small, self-contained, one-person computer games, i.e., baseball or football, etc. In addition, try to arrange to have a TV with a cartridge game, such as is made by Atari or Coleco. It is likely that several members of your congregation have home computers, for instance, Radio Shack, Atari, Apple, Texas Instruments, Commodore, etc. You might invite a computer owner to bring his or her computer and join in your session for the day, giving instruction in its use. Perhaps you can even arrange to have more than one computer available.

Think about ways you might decorate your room for the next four sessions. Find pictures of electronic devices in magazines and newspapers and bring these with you. Your early arrivals might help by putting them around the room or beginning a collage. A question such as "What are these used for?" or "What would life be like without this?" can be printed on construction paper and posted under a group of pictures. Bring a supply of used computer printouts to hang on the walls, as previously suggested.

If you have a chalkboard, copy drawings of satellite dishes, satellites, and robots—or use newsprint or computer printer paper. You've probably got an eager artist who would come early to do this.

Before the Group Arrives

Arrange your room with several tables spaced as widely as possible, so that children can move from one activity to another. On these tables place the video games, computer, etc.

Beginning Activity

Enjoying Modern Technology (40-60 minutes)

Your role during this period will vary, depending on the ways in which your class is accustomed to interacting. As children arrive, you may want to direct them to available games. Intervene, if necessary, to insure that all have a time with the more popular activities. It is hoped that you will also participate in the games and allow the children to teach you the finer points of Pac-man or whatever! Children may get very excited about using computers. Your role may also be to help them share and work together in teams or small groups.

Developing Activities

Sharing Impressions (10-15 minutes)

Bring the group together and invite discussion about the activity time. If your schedule permits, allow time to talk about favorite games and impressions of the computer. Ask the young people to name all of the ways they can think of that electronic devices are used in the modern world. Obvious answers will come quickly, especially various uses of the computer, since the games will be fresh in everyone's memory. Prompt the discussion with mention of the use of electronic devices in their homes. (For example, electronic controls in microwave ovens, and digital clocks and readouts in coffee makers.) Another question you might want to ask is, "What, to you, is the most important invention or product to come out in the past year?"

Closing Activity

Where Did It All Come from? (10-15 minutes)

There are a couple of good reasons for ending this session with a brief look at the creative activity of God. The Bible is an ancient book, of course, and children (and many adults for that matter) may feel that there is little connection between the ancient records of God's creative activity and the accomplishments of a host of brilliant engineers and scientists. Did God only establish a basic foundation, with everything else being the work of human beings?

Another reason for this suggested closing is in the negative reactions that children may have sensed from church-related adults to electronic technology as they know it best in the video game. Their schools have probably made some real efforts to use computers as teaching aids in the classroom, while this is generally not true in most church school classes. Although the computer may not be as functional in your group as in the public school, the subtle impressions gained by children could be that there is a gulf between Christian faith and modern technology. For this reason we suggest that you close with this grateful affirmation that modern technology is one of God's good gifts.

To enable children to reach some of these conclusions, ask each to choose one of the following passages to find and read: Genesis 1:1-26; John 1:1-3; and Exodus 31:1-11.

Have the children think about such questions as: Who created the world? Where did people get the power and skill to use what is in the world? Who gives people the knowledge they need for building and discovering new things?

After a few minutes of this kind of discussion, you might explain that the Exodus passage tells how the Israelites were commanded to build the tabernacle to God's specifications but had no doubt lost the needed skills during the long Egyptian captivity. Now these abilities are restored. God is seen again as the source of skill, ability, and knowledge in all kinds of crafts. Not only is God the Creator of all, but God is also the giver of the genius that has allowed humankind to "work" electrons even as artisans of old worked gold and fabric.

As you close, raise the question with the group about the origins of all these very interesting and powerful electronic devices. Where did they come from? Who invented them? Who taught the inventors? Read John 1:1-3 with the group as a way to summarize the idea that God is the source of things and ideas.

Suggest that technical devices are a result of the creative minds God has given us and are things over which we have been called to give wise stewardship. Close with the singing or reading of the hymn, "How Beautiful Is the Green Earth."

Alternate Activity

You may have some students who would be willing to do research over the next three weeks on a topic of current interest in electronics. If you browse the local magazine rack, you will find several popularly written science, computer, and electronics magazines out of which a report could be presented. Some suggested topics would be: fiber optics, direct broadcasting from satellite, Teletext, new video games, robotics, and new uses of computers. Fiber optics is a rapidly developing technology of transmitting vast amounts of information over glass fibers rather than wires. Direct broadcast from satellite is a system that will eventually provide programming to individual home "dishes" that might be as small as three feet (one meter) in diameter. Teletext is one system for obtaining information from a central computer using the home TV set. Plan for one brief report each week. The school or public library should have the necessary current science magazines.

> **Bible Used in This Session**: Genesis 1:1-26; John 1:1-3 and Exodus 31:1-11

Session 2

The World of Jesus and My World

Purpose

- To examine the ways Jesus related to persons and discover what he valued about relationships.
- To compare Jesus' world and my world and what was/is valued in each.

Background for Leader(s)

In thinking about the two worlds it is important to realize that the issues we will be exploring are not those of the ancient world versus the modern world. One of the most important things you can do in this unit is to explore with your class the timeless choices between caring for *things* and caring for *people*. As was suggested earlier, the difference which the passing centuries and the technological discoveries of our era have made is that it is now so much easier to use *things* to avoid relationships.

Another challenge facing you is that of supporting the best of the modern world and its advances while calling into judgment the loss of sensitivity that can come to persons who retreat into a world of machines. Remember the suggested closing for the previous session. Can you build on that positive base while comparing Jesus' values with some contemporary ones?

The computer has added some new dynamics to these age-old choices of caring for persons and caring for things. Computers are logical and precise and are always ready to respond to the user's commands. (Well, almost always!) They don't pass judgments, and they work willingly and silently at the most boring tasks. As we well know, people are not like that! Persons are demanding, get emotional, and have their own ideas about how things ought to be done. Someone has suggested that persons enjoy losing themselves at the computer because that might be the only place in their lives where they have a sense of "being in charge."

On the other hand, Jesus made himself available to people with few reservations. The ones who were held at a distance were those who wanted to defend their righteousness or play entrapment games. The Bible passages suggested for your study are representative of many that will come to your mind as you prepare.

Getting Ready

The computer pictures, paper, and other decorations you used last week should stay in place for the entire unit. Try to find some pictures of robots to place on the wall with appropriate questions that will direct attention to them, such as "What is this used for?" and "Can you think of an interesting name for this one?" You can find robot pictures in science and electronic magazines and possibly in the ads from companies such as Heathkit, which markets a robot in kit form. Also check the brochures from automobile dealers, since so much auto production is now done with robots.

You will need number badges for each class member for the suggested beginning activity. These can be made from half sheets of construction paper. Attach a string to the paper so it can be hung around the neck. Prepare the numbers (6-8 digits in length) in the style of optically scannable numerals (like those strange ones you see along the bottom of your checks). Place a second copy of each number on a small slip of paper in a box for random choosing. The purpose of this activity is to experience, in a small way, the depersonalization that can come with being only known as a number.

If someone in your church has a computer and has done some simple programming, you may want to add some reality by using this alternate activity. Ask the computer owner to bring the equipment to class and write a random number-generating program to assign the children to various activities. This will require some extra work and planning but will add to the class's interest in the session. You will also need some large sheets of newsprint or unburst sections of computer printer paper for the robot designs.

Beginning Activity

Is This Really Me? (10-15 minutes)

As children arrive, give each a number and, from this point on, have everyone address others only by their numbers. Call the group together by numbers ("#____ through ____ will gather in a circle.") Make these as commands rather than requests.

Make assignments or ask questions without regard to the sex or interests of the class member. The following are some suggestions for this opening period:

#____, measure the height of #____ and #____ and report.

#____, tell us how many are in your family.

#____, find out who has the most pets.
#____, how many dresses do you have?
#____, get everyone's shoe size and report the average.

Choose persons to answer the questions by drawing the numbers from the box. You might also want to have fun together by asking questions that will obviously not fit the person. Bring this activity to a close by commenting that, because you used only numbers when calling on persons to answer questions, the questions sometimes didn't fit the person. Point out that there's much more to be known about each other than how tall we are or what is our average shoe size.

Developing Activities

The Perfect Robot (20-30 minutes)

For this next activity assign work groups of two or three, using numbers drawn randomly from the box. Give each group large sheets of paper and markers and ask that they draw what they consider to be the perfect robot. These pictures will be posted about the room and kept until next week. Ask each group to put explanatory comments alongside the features of their drawing.

Call the group together again, and allow each group to describe their work. Comment on the general nature of computers and robots: they don't make mistakes, they obey, they are logical, feelings don't affect their decisions etc. Call for a brief discussion of what they can't do: be friendly, care, be sympathetic, understand people's hurts, etc. Use this as an entry into the Bible study.

Jesus Showed the Way (25-40 minutes)

The following list contains only a few of the many Scriptures that you might use to explore the way Jesus related to people or how he taught about relationships:

Luke 10:38-42—Visit with Mary and Martha
John 20:11-18—Jesus appears to Mary
Matthew 8:1-3; 14-15; 9:27-30—Jesus healing people
Mark 14:12-21—Passover with the disciples
Luke 9:10-17—Feeding five thousand people
Luke 10:25-37—Parable of the good Samaritan
Luke 18:15-17—Jesus and the children

Divide the class into work groups again (you may choose to use the same groupings as in the robot drawing) and assign these passages to each group. You will have some sense of how well your people read and how easily they participate in research activities, and this will determine whether you will need to add additional passages.

Provide markers and paper and ask each group to read the Bible passages together and to decide how to describe the ways Jesus treated people. Ask each group to make a list of these descriptions. Remind the class that you have talked about how easy it is to treat others as things or to wish they were more like machines and robots.

Allow time for a general class sharing of the groups' findings. Have each group post its list on the wall and share with the total class. Draw attention to similar descriptions and summarize, adding from your own study of these passages or others that you have used as background reading. If some groups are having trouble getting started, the following descriptions might serve as seed thoughts:

—enjoying friendship
—going out of his way to help someone in need
—willing to touch people whom others thought unclean
—open to people whom others thought unimportant, such as children
—willing to take time to fulfill basic needs such as hunger
—settled an argument with a gentle rebuke
—acted to strengthen Mary's faith
—forgave persons who did wrong

Alternate Activity (5 minutes)

Invite one of those who have prepared a report on a topic of particular interest to present it to the class.

Closing Activity (5 minutes)

Draw attention to the work the young people have placed on the walls: the robots and the lists from the Bible study. Remind the group that treating people like things is not a new problem but is as old as the human race. Comment on the problems that are unique to our world and how electronics can make it very easy for us to be isolated from others. Lead the group in a prayer of thanks for Jesus' example.

Bible Used in This Session: Luke 10:38-42; John 20:11-18; Matthew 8:1-3, 14-15; 9:27-30; Mark 14:12-21; Luke 9:10-17; Luke 10:25-37; Luke 18:15-17

Session 3

How Do I Choose?

Purpose

- To help children see ways to choose how to use their time.
- To help children explore ways they can use electronics and yet maintain a balance between their relationships and their other interests.

Background for Leader(s)

The world of electronics is like a fast-breaking news story. There is a continual flow of new developments to amaze, excite, and perhaps frighten people of all ages. A very appropriate byword for our age is, ''If it's on the shelf, it's already out of date!''

You will note that the word ''balance'' is used in the suggested purposes for this session. In the previous two sessions of this unit we have endeavored to have some good experiences with modern technology and then examine the importance of relationships, particularly as they were modeled for us by Jesus. This session will continue to help the class develop an appreciation for the wonders of technology and in addition raise the issue of a balanced life. As the child becomes overly enamored of computers, TV, and electronic games, he or she may push aside other people and other creative outlets.

It might be well to remind ourselves again of the more subtle dangers that can accompany immersion in a world of machines. Some writers have expressed the concern that the logic, cold obedience, and predictability of the computer can cause one to expect the same of people and may lead to a style of life that places less importance on feelings.

Do you normally read articles in the newspapers and magazines about technological developments? As you have prepared for this unit, have you done any extra research to make yourself aware of the radical changes that are taking place, particularly in communications? Technological advancement is one of those ''mixed blessings,'' for the technology we have been exploring with the children can not only inhibit communication but also enable it. Getting in touch with someone is easier because of the computer and electronics. This unit of this book, for instance, is being written on a computer using a very powerful word processor. It is being stored on a plastic disk as magnetic impulses which could easily be sent to the editor over the phone lines through another computer late at night for recovery the next day. So by means of electronics you and I are touching—but how personal is it?

The opening activity is suggested to force some value choices and involve the group in discussion. The assignment may be duplicated for each student or (if necessary) placed on newsprint or the chalkboard. The time charts used in the last activity may also be prepared before the session begins. If you can make duplicate copies, draw seven columns on an 8½-by-11-inch (21.8-by-28.2-cm) sheet, add day-of-the-week headings, and divide the chart horizontally into Morning, Afternoon, and Evening sections. If you cannot make copies, have each child fold an 8½-by-11 piece of paper into eight columns (fold in half three times). You will have an extra column in which children can put their names and the words ''Morning,'' ''Afternoon,'' and ''Evening.''

My Time Chart

Name	Sun	Mon	Tues	Wed	Thur	Fri	Sat
Morning							
Afternoon							
Evening							

Beginning Activities (10-15 minutes)

As the children arrive, have them work individually on the following assignment: ''Word has come over TV and radio that a swarm of killer bees will arrive in your community in ten minutes, and you must be prepared to leave immediately. You will be allowed to take three personal items with you (food and water are already taken care of). Write down the three items.''

Allow about five minutes for individual work, and then form groups of three to decide on a list for the whole group. Try to keep a spirit of hurry and good fun during this activity.

Bring the groups together to share quickly their lists. Raise some of the following questions for discussion: Why did you choose these things? What different opinions did your group have? What gives things different value or importance to you? (Suggest factors such as price, sentiment, dependence on you for care, value to someone else, relationship, life . . . if the group needs some seed thoughts.)

14

Developing Activities

Four People Who Made Choices (20-30 minutes)

Suggest to the group that there are many Bible stories of people who made choices based on different values. In small groups or as a total group, have children read the following three passages, sharing brief comments and questions after each story:

—Mary and·Martha (Luke 10:38-42). There was certainly nothing wrong with preparing dinner for a guest! Why was Mary complimented? Sometimes being with a friend and learning can be more important than performing traditionally expected tasks.

—The Rich Young Ruler (Matthew 19:16-22). He was obviously a good man. Why did Jesus want him to give his money away? Is it important to be poor? Does everyone need to give all his or her money away? The rich young ruler was placing too much value on his wealth and for him becoming a follower of Jesus meant making hard choices about having lots of money.

—Jesus and Zacchaeus (Luke 19:1-10). Why did Zacchaeus offer to give his money away? If you could ask him what is the most important thing in the world, what do you think he might say?

All of these people struggled with finding the valuable or important things in life. Their ideas of what this meant for them were quite different.

God's Gift of Time—How Do I Spend It? (15-25 minutes)

Suggest to the class that, while they may not be a "Martha," a "Rich Young Ruler," or a "Zacchaeus," they too are called to make similar value choices. Time is one commodity that everyone gets to spend. Everyone's day has twenty-four hours!

Hand out the time charts which you prepared or ask the boys and girls to prepare their own as described in the introduction to this session. Ask each to work individually in filling in the kinds of things they might do in a typical week (or in three or four days, if a week will take too long). Ask for a guess on the amounts of time they will spend on free-choice activities such as hobbies, playing with friends, playing alone with computer or video games, reading, TV watching, talking on the phone, etc.

After they have completed their charts, ask them to share what seems to take up most of their time apart from school. What interests other than computers or video games do the children have? Invite some general discussion of what a balanced week for a person of that age ought to include. Also discuss the answer to the following questions: Would the idea of balance allow for some activities being more important than others?

Alternate Activities (5 to 20 minutes)

1. (5 minutes) Have a person who has prepared a report share it with the group.

2. (20 minutes) Today's session would be an ideal time to have someone from your church family share the way in which he or she makes choices in the use of time. It is important that the group be encouraged to explore traditional crafts and hobbies. Consider inviting one or more persons who have developed creative hobbies to show their work and speak on the importance of a wide range of creative interests and hobbies. Plan for this presentation to be a demonstration rather than a mere discussion. For instance, a person who does woodworking as a hobby could bring in something she or he made, and some tools used in the craft. Or a person who does community service could bring in posters, letters, or pamphlets used to promote an issue or community service. Playing electronic games, while challenging to hand-and-eye coordination, is generally not an outlet for creativity, but writing a game program certainly could be. As a result of this sharing by others, your group may be willing to share their hobbies in a future session.

3. (20 minutes) Have the group role-play the following situation and discuss possible variations on the ending:

"You are deeply involved in playing your favorite video game and you have finally mastered it well enough to move on to the next level of difficulty. You have been playing for 45 minutes and your thumb is sore, but you want to continue. The doorbell rings, and your mother tells you that it is one of your good friends. Her/his family is waiting in the car and you are invited to go to the local shopping mall with them."

Play this three or four times, with different persons in the role of game player, mother, and friend. Add reality to it by having the friend state that he/she wanted you to come along for company because it promises to be a boring time. Discuss the issues and particularly the feelings each character has. Have the group suggest possible dialogue and the reasons for a particular course of action.

Closing Activity (5 minutes)

Ask the group members to bring in their electronic games (and computers, if possible) for the next session.

Lead the group in a prayer of thanks for each day's opportunities to make wise choices. Pray together for the strength to follow Jesus' example.

> **Bible Used in This Session:** Luke 10:38-42; Matthew 19:16-22; Luke 19:1-10

Session 4

Violence—What Is It? What to Do About It

Purpose

- To help children to explore the issue of violence, to recognize it, and to see what it does to relationships.
- To help children to identify areas of and kinds of violence and explore alternatives.

Background for Leader(s)

In the days of comic books, the words filling the scene were "Zap," "Bam," "Pow," "Kaboom," as the good guys and the bad guys went at it with fists, guns, tanks, spaceships, and a wide variety of other weaponry. Now you can walk past the arcade or the television and see those same frames in living color and action and hear the varied sounds of mayhem as well.

Violence is hardly a new concern. The reasons for our being attracted to the attack of one living thing on another must be strangely and deeply rooted in sin within us. Long before the days of television, ordinary people showed up at Roman circuses to see gladiators kill each other and lions devour Christians. Witch drownings in colonial America always drew a crowd, and a hanging in the Old West was a community event. In Dickens' classic *Tale of Two Cities* the crowds lined the streets as the carts full of prisoners rumbled on their way to the guillotine, and Mme. Defarge knitted and philosophized as the spectacle went on. Why do boxing matches attract much larger audiences than tennis tournaments? Why does professional wrestling bring an audience to a fever pitch and a chess tournament does not?

This one brief session with your group can hardly do more than scratch the surface of this issue. Give attention again to the suggested goals for this session. It is certainly appropriate for you to rework these to describe better the outcomes you are working toward with your group. One part of the issue is the effect that observing violence can have on relationships. Obviously, violent behavior destroys relationships, but there is also the concern that "spectator violence" might have a very subtle but definite effect on persons.

Antisocial behavior on television has gotten a lot of attention in recent years. At least one court case was widely publicized in which the defendant claimed to have been criminally motivated by scenes from television. Many careful studies have been documented which have attempted to find correlations between viewers' behavior and dramatized antisocial scenes. These studies show children's behavior is affected negatively, although people with a pro-television bias may want to ignore the implications. You can find interesting descriptions of many of these research studies in materials which are mentioned in the Resources section of the unit introduction. While the probability that persons will run out to duplicate something seen on the tube is not supported, the concern remains that we will all be gradually desensitized by vicarious participation in that which is standard fare on television and in video games. Games are mentioned here because, as you know, these are very much a part of the children's world. While the games are much less personal than a television program, many deal with winning by destroying an enemy.

It is suggested that you bring back to class this week the electronic games that you used earlier. The first activity suggested is a time of playing with these games again so that they will be very fresh in everyone's mind as you talk about them. You may introduce the game in this book if you did not get it ready in time for the first session in this unit. It is found on pages 19-22. Try to have some games available that have the challenge of destroying a living enemy, rather than just a baseball game or a downhill race.

Your usual television schedule may not include any of the shows that your group members see. Ask a couple of children early in the week what they watch and make a point to see these programs yourself. In this way you'll have some very current information to add to the discussion.

If you have already used the unit "The Things That Make for Peace" (see pages 23-36), this discussion of games related to war and violence may be a review. It may also bring new insights.

Before the Group Arrives

Arrange the room as you did for the first session, with work tables for groups and individuals to play and demonstrate the video and electronic games that they have brought. Put some of the sounds and phrases that you have heard during this past week from violent television shows, on the chalkboard, or on newsprint around the room. Typical examples would be sentences like "I'll blow you away," and "Stand back or your partner gets it."

Beginning Activity

Game Playing (10 minutes)

Allow a few minutes for play with the games which have been brought. If you were not able to have the games available, go directly to the next activity.

The World of Games and Television (20-30 minutes)

Place the following chart headings on the board or newsprint:

Name of Game	Goal of the Game
1.	
2.	
3.	
Show or Movie	Plot
1.	
2.	
3.	

Invite group members to discuss the games that they have been playing and decide what the goal of each game is (e.g., kill Klingons, cross the river, find the treasure, etc.). Expand the discussion to include their favorite arcade and home video games as well, and list these. Begin a second list using favorite television shows and movies, gathering the same information on each one. Give particular attention to those which you watched these past weeks which had violent scenes.

Comment on the concerns about violence in games and on television that many people are raising. Ask the group to look back over the two lists that they have developed and to point out the ones that contain some kind of violence. Take a quick poll, trying to reach some agreement on ranking the four most violent games and shows. Try to keep this discussion spirited and moving quite rapidly. Ask members to describe their feelings as they watch these shows or play the games. Do you like to watch make-believe gun battles? How do you feel when you watch a well-staged fight? Do you feel any different when you see killing or fighting on the news?

Invite some general discussion on the question, "What is violence?" After the more obvious "physical" answers, try to move the class to consider some of the more subtle ways in which people do harm to each other. Comment on the fact that many of the games and shows set up an "enemy" who is to be destroyed, or at least hated and feared. Raise the following questions with the group and invite brief discussion:

What makes someone an enemy in real life?
Why do people hurt others?
Think of a time when someone purposely hurt you or you purposely hurt someone else. What kinds of feelings did you have toward each other?

Developing Activities

Bible Study of The Good Samaritan (15 minutes)

The children may be familiar with this good Samaritan parable and the contrasts that are usually drawn to teach the meaning of love for one's neighbor. This is also a story of two different kinds of violence. The more obvious is that of the robbers and their seriously wounding the hapless traveler. The other is the more subtle "not caring" that speaks to some of the concerns that we are attempting to explore in this study. The priest and the Levite had not been hardened by watching television or even the Roman circuses, but had somehow become hardened enough so that they could justify walking by without helping the wounded human being. While this is only a story, it is gripping because it is so realistic. When Jesus told it, it was an age when gladiators killed each other in professional sport. Criminals were hung on crosses in public areas as a lesson to everyone, so that in a short time a crowd could call gleefully for Jesus' crucifixion. It is no wonder that this kind of violence could cause the priest and Levite to turn away in revulsion, or relish it, or simply ignore it.

Some years ago there was an incident reported in New York that has become quite famous. A young woman was attacked in a parking lot, and her cries attracted persons in the surrounding apartment buildings who watched from their windows but did nothing. There's no way of knowing the feelings of these spectators or the factors which led to their noninvolvement. There is, however, a deep concern that continual viewing of violence through the distance and impersonality of television in particular might lead to a lessening of sensitivity and caring.

Read the good Samaritan story (Luke 10:25-37) to the class and direct attention to the characters other than the Samaritan. Divide the group into threes and give each group newsprint and markers. Place the following drawing on the board and ask the groups to duplicate it and write along the arrows the feelings that each person in this story might have had for each other one.

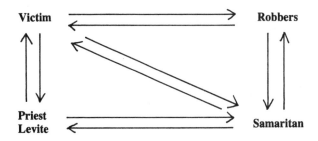

17

Ask the group to comment on the reasons why it might have been easy for the priest and Levite to leave the victim without help. Add your own thoughts from your understanding of cruelty in the ancient world.

Take Action (10-15 minutes)

Suggest to the group that they may want to influence the amount of violence in electronic games and on television. They might like to begin by making other church members aware of the problem, since some similarities may be seen between the priest and Levite and modern church people.

Here are two suggestions which may be carried out in a brief time:

1. Children may make posters for display at church which ask people to write letters to the editor of the local newspaper or to the local television station, protesting violence in video games and television.

2. The group may compose an item for the church newsletter or Sunday bulletin about violence in the media and popular games.

The children themselves may write letters to the editor of the local newspaper or local television station to raise the consciousness of church members and the public at large. If the letter also included artwork, it might attract more attention from the person receiving it.

Alternate Activity (20 minutes)

Draw attention to the list of video games that the group has developed and rated according to the amount of violence contained in them. Comment on the fact that there are many favorite games that do not use violence for excitement. Direct attention to the lists that you developed earlier of the ways Jesus valued people. Suggest the challenge of designing a computer game that will be fun and that will also include the positive values that you have shared. Divide the class into small work groups and ask each to develop an outline of a game (characters, goal, how to score points, how many players, etc.). Suggest features such as rescuing rather than destroying, or preparing for natural disasters to try to keep a city safe, if the groups need prompting.

Closing Activities (5 minutes)

Share your concern that persons today not become so accustomed to violence on television shows and on the news that they become like the priest and Levite in the story—able to walk by someone in need without caring. Suggest that the members of the group identify their feelings as they watch television this week.

Close with prayer asking God's help in maintaining loving, caring relationships.

Bible Used in This Session: Luke 10:25-37

BIBLE KNOWLEDGE

A Learning Game from the Bible

To the Teacher

This study game provides players with a study of both the Old Testament and the New Testament. An individual may play alone or small groups of students may play in place of the one or two players noted in the game. Have several Bibles available for your students. If a student answers a question incorrectly, the computer will ask the student to look up the correct answer in a Bible. The computer will not proceed with the game until the correct answer is given.

The questions are asked in a manner that will capture the interest of students by using such paraphrases as "She led an army" and "He built a great temple." As the teacher, you may want to be familiar with the Scripture passages these questions are based on as you discuss the stories with your students. If you do not know where the passage may be found for a particular question, deliberately give an incorrect answer to the computer and the computer will display where the passage may be found in the Bible.

It's personal. It's fun. It's solid Bible study.

The game is written in a very simple form of BASIC. This will allow it to be run on the following computers: Commodore 64, Texas Instruments 99/4A, TRS–80, Apple II, and Atari.

Created by Daniel Holland. © 1984 Educational Ministries, American Baptist Churches in the U.S.A. Used by permission.

READY,

```
10 GOSUB 20:GOTO 100
20 REM ROUTINE TO CLEAR SCREEN
30 FOR N=1 TO 20:PRINT:NEXT
40 RETURN
100 REM WELCOME AND INSTRUCTIONS
101 PRINT "     **** BIBLE KNOWLEDGE ****"
102 PRINT"    A LEARNING GAME FROM THE BIBLE"
103 PRINT"      CREATED BY DANIEL HOLLAND"
104 PRINT"COPYRIGHT: EDUCATIONAL MINISTERIES 1984"
105 PRINT"AMERICAN BAPTIST CHURCHES,VALLEY FORGE  PA. 19482-0851"
106 X=6000:GOSUB 107
107 FOR I=1 TO X
108 NEXT I
109 PRINT:PRINT:PRINT:PRINT
110 PRINT"WELCOME TO THE BIBLE KNOWLEDGE"
120 PRINT"COMPUTER GAME,  YOU WILL HAVE A"
130 PRINT"SERIES OF MULTIPLE-CHOICE"
140 PRINT"QUESTIONS WITH THREE CHOICES,"
150 PRINT"GIVE YOUR FIRST NAME(S) AND"
160 PRINT"THE NUMBER OF PLAYERS, THEN "
170 PRINT"CHOOSE OLD OR NEW TESTAMENT"
180 PRINT"QUESTIONS,  YOU WILL GET TWO "
190 PRINT"POINTS FOR A CORRECT ANSWER"
200 PRINT"AND IF YOU ANSWER INCORRECTLY"

210 PRINT"A CHANCE TO FIND THE ANSWER"
220 PRINT"FOR ONE POINT,"
230 PRINT:PRINT
240 PRINT"PRESS THE 'ENTER' OR 'RETURN"
250 PRINT"KEY EACH TIME YOU GIVE AN "
260 PRINT"ANSWER TO TELL THE COMPUTER"
270 PRINT"TO GO AHEAD "
280 PRINT:PRINT "USE CAPITAL LETTERS  "
290 PRINT:PRINT
500 REM CHOICES
510 INPUT "READY?..(PRESS 'RETURN' OR 'ENTER) "; G
520 GOSUB 20
530 INPUT" ONE OR TWO PLAYERS?  ";P
540 IF P<1 OR P>2 THEN GOTO 530
550 IF P=2 THEN GOTO 580
560 INPUT" YOUR FIRST NAME? ";P1$
570 GOTO 610
580 INPUT" FIRST PLAYER? ";P1$
590 PRINT:INPUT" SECOND PLAYER? ";P2$
600 PRINT:PRINT
610 INPUT "OLD OR NEW TESTMENT? (TYPE O OR N) ";X$
620 IF X$="N" OR X$="O" THEN GOTO 640
630 GOTO 610
640 GOSUB 20
650 REM GET DATA ROUTINE
660 P3=1
670 READ Q$
680 IF Q$="END" THEN GOTO 1500
690 READ A1$,A2$,A3$,B$,C,T$
700 IF T$=X$ THEN GOTO 720
```

```
710 GOTO 670
720 IF P3=1 THEN P3$=P1$
730 IF P=1 THEN P3=1: GOTO 780
740 IF P3=2 THEN P3$=P2$:P3=0
750 P3=P3+1
760 PRINT;P3$;" ,YOUR TURN,,"
770 PRINT:PRINT
780 PRINT Q$;":"
790 PRINT TAB(10);"1  ";A1$
800 PRINT TAB(10);"2  ";A2$
810 PRINT TAB(10);"3  ";A3$
820 PRINT:PRINT
830 INPUT"YOUR ANSWER (1,2 OR 3),,";A
840 PRINT:PRINT
850 IF A<1 OR A>3 THEN GOTO 830
860 IF A=C THEN S=2:GOSUB 2010:GOTO 670
1000 REM WRONG ANSWER ROUTINE
1010 PRINT:PRINT
1020 PRINT"SORRY, WRONG ANSWER, YOU CAN"
1030 PRINT"LOOK IT UP IN ";B$
1040 PRINT:PRINT
1050 INPUT"ENTER CORRECT ANSWER,,";A
1060 IF A<1 OR A>3 THEN GOTO 1050
1070 IF A=C THEN S=1:GOSUB 2010:GOTO 670
1080 PRINT"WRONG AGAIN, NEXT QUESTION"
1090 INPUT"PRESS RETURN,,,";G
1100 GOSUB 20
1110 GOTO 670
1500 REM END ROUTINE
1510 GOSUB 20
1520 PRINT"THANKS FOR PLAYING"
1530 PRINT P1$;",  YOUR SCORE,,,";S1
1540 IF P=1 THEN GOTO 1580
1550 PRINT P2$;",  YOUR SCORE,,,";S2
1560 PRINT:PRINT:PRINT
1570 PRINT" YOUR COMBINED SCORE,,,"S1+S2
1580 RESTORE:S1=0:S2=0:S3=0
1590 PRINT:PRINT:PRINT
1600 INPUT"ANOTHER GAME? (Y OR N)";G$
1610 IF G$="Y" THEN GOTO 520
1620 GOSUB 20:PRINT"....BYE,,,,"
1630 END
2000 REM SCORING LOOP
2010 IF P3$=P1$ THEN S1=S1+S:S3=S1
2020 IF P3$=P2$ THEN S2=S2+S:S3=S2
2030 PRINT" RIGHT, ";P3$;"; TOTAL= ";S3
2040 PRINT:PRINT
2050 INPUT"PRESS RETURN WHEN READY,,";G
2060 GOSUB 20:RETURN
3000 REM DATA BASE
3010 DATA "HE TOOK A BOAT RIDE"
3020 DATA"JONAH","MICAH","EZRA"
3030 DATA"JONAH 1:2",1,"O"
3040 DATA"NAME JACOB'S BROTHER,,"
3050 DATA"ISAAC","ESAU","ISHMAEL"
3060 DATA"GENESIS 25:24-26",2,"O"
3070 DATA "HOW MANY DISCIPLES?"
3080 DATA "11","12","14"
3090 DATA"MARK 3:13-19",2,"N"
3100 DATA"OLD TEST,-HOW MANY BOOKS?"
```

```
3110 DATA"27","38","39","CONTENTS",3,"O"
3120 DATA"NEW TEST,-HOW MANY BOOKS?"
3130 DATA"27","26","29","CONTENTS",1,"N"
3140 DATA"TEN COMMANDMENTS GIVEN AT?"
3150 DATA"MT,SINAI","MT,NEBO","MT,EGYPT"
3160 DATA"EXODUS 19:20",1,"O"
3170 DATA"A NEIGHBOR STORY JESUS TOLD"
3180 DATA"PRODIGAL SON","UNJUST STEWARD"
3190 DATA"GOOD SAMARITAN"
3200 DATA"LUKE 10:25-38",3,"N"
3210 DATA"WHICH BOOK DID PAUL WRITE?"
3220 DATA"ACTS","ROMANS","REVELATION"
3230 DATA"EPHESIANS 1:1",2,"N"
3240 DATA"WHO WAS JOSEPH'S FATHER?"
3250 DATA"JACOB","ABRAHAM","ISAIAH"
3260 DATA"GENESIS 30:19-26",1,"O"
3270 DATA"SHE LED A VICTORY PARADE,,"
3280 DATA"MIRIAM","DOROTHY","JEZEBEL"
3290 DATA"EXODUS 15:19-21",1,"O"
3300 DATA"HE BUILT A GREAT TEMPLE"
3310 DATA"DAVID","SOLOMON","ISAIAH"
3320 DATA"1 KINGS 6:37-38",2,"O"
3330 DATA"HE PLAYED A HARP AND SANG"
3340 DATA"JOEL","NIMROD","DAVID"
3350 DATA"1 SAMUEL 16:19-23",3,"O"
3360 DATA"THIS WOMAN LED AN ARMY"
3370 DATA"RUTH","DEBORAH","ESTHER"
3380 DATA"JUDGES 4:4-10",2,"O"
3390 DATA"HE KNEW A KING'S DREAM"
3400 DATA"JEREMIAH","DANIEL","HOSEA"
3410 DATA"DANIEL 2:24-28",2,"O"
3420 DATA"WEAR THE ? OF RIGHTEOUSNESS"
3430 DATA"CLOAK","BREASTPLATE","HELMET"
3440 DATA"EPHESIANS 6:13-18",2,"N"
3450 DATA"SHE SAW JESUS AS A BABY"
3460 DATA"PRISCILLA","ANNA","HANNAH"
3470 DATA"LUKE 2:36",2,"N"
3480 DATA"END"
```

The Things That Make for Peace

by Betty Grant

Unit Introduction

In Romans 14:19 (KJV), the apostle Paul says, "Let us therefore follow after the things which make for peace. . . ." This admonition is very seldom heard in our world. Nations and people compete and "follow after" the things that make for ill will and strife and wars, but very few people are willing to do as Paul suggested.

In that section of Romans, Paul is talking about being willing to surrender some of our freedoms, some of our habits, some of our desires in order to make peace among all people. That is the kind of surrender which peacemaking requires. Peacemaking requires deliberate attempts to make peace.

Too often we think of peace as something passive—no wars. However, real peace is active. It not only means no war or fighting; it also means taking positive actions to bring about peace and goodwill among all people. This is what this unit is all about: learning those positive steps which make for peace.

This unit is concerned primarily with peace in the everyday, real-life situations in which children find themselves— home, school, and play. There are very few suggestions for peacemaking at the world level. Rather, through these studies, perhaps children will learn "the things that make for peace" in their own situations, and perhaps these learnings may be transferred to peacemaking on the world arena.

Peacemaking is a Bible-centered activity and concern. Almost all church people remember Jesus' seventh beatitude in Matthew 5:9 (KJV), "Blessed are the peacemakers, for they shall be called the children of God." Throughout the Scriptures peace is a major concern. A quick look at a concordance will show many references to peace and peacemaking. These sessions attempt to capture some of this biblical concern in fresh ways, so that children may begin to practice peacemaking at home, school, play, and wherever they may be.

In the first session we will consider how helping to affirm people—"building up" people—may provide a foundation for peace. Too often peace among people is lost through catty remarks, and put-downs. If we can begin to affirm others as people created in God's image, perhaps we can begin to live at peace with them.

The second session is concerned with communication. Having affirmed the God-given personhood of all people, we then move to facilitate communication. Peace is sometimes lost because people are not communicating, even when they are shouting at one another!

In the third session we move on to the next step in peacemaking, which is learning to cooperate rather than compete with others. When we affirm the God-given personhood of each human being and really work at communication, then we will be ready for cooperation with others.

The fourth session accepts realistically that even the best intentioned people sometimes face conflict situations. And so, in Session 4 we will experience some ways to resolve conflicts peacefully.

Finally, we move toward commitment to peacemaking in the fifth session.

The educational methodology of this unit is based on what someone has called the "discovery approach." That is, the sessions are planned to get the children involved in activities and discussion so that they may experience and discover for themselves the things that make for peace. While some background material for each session is provided for leaders, the sessions are not intended to be "input" times in which the teacher or leader simply *tells* the children about peace. We hope the children will begin to *discover* how they may become peacemakers.

Materials to Have Ready

You probably have readily available such items as pencils, paper, scissors, Bibles. Before the first session of this unit, you may want to gather certain other specific items:

Session 1: • straight pins or masking tape
  • *Crow Boy*, a storybook by Taro Yashima
  • copies of an outline drawing of a T-shirt
Session 2: • magazines, scissors, glue, construction paper
Session 3: • circles cut into puzzles (see pages 30-31)
  • construction paper and art supplies
  • fruit salad ingredients and utensils

Session 4: • rhythm instruments, if available
  • pancakes or crackers
  • cups for juice or water
Session 5: • streamers or scarves
  • recorded music
  • several kinds of paper
  • waxed paper, warm iron
  • contact paper, permanent markers, string, coat hangers

Resources for Use by Leaders

Allen, T. Harrell, "To Accept All Feelings," *The Christian Home*, vol. 10, no. 7, March 1978, pp. 18-19.

Bodenhamer, Gretchen; Burger, M. Leonard; Prutzman, Priscilla; and Stern, Lee. *The Friendly Classroom for a Small Planet.* Wayne, N.J.: Avery Publishing Group, Inc., 1978.

Fluegelman, Andrew, *More New Games.* New York: Doubleday & Co., Inc., 1981.

Judson, Stephanie, ed. *A Manual on Nonviolence and Children.* Philadelphia: Friends Peace Committee, 1977.

McGinnis, Kathleen and James, *Parenting for Peace and Justice.* Maryknoll, N.Y.: Orbis Books, 1983.

Orlick, Terry, *The Cooperative Sports and Games Book.* New York: Pantheon Books, Inc., 1978.

Smith, Judy Gattis, *Developing a Child's Spiritual Growth Through Sight, Sound, Taste, Touch & Smell.* Nashville: Abingdon Press, 1983.

Try This: Family Adventures Toward Shalom (Created by the Ecumenical Task Force on Christian Education for World Peace). Nashville: Discipleship Resources, 1979.

Resources for Use by Children

Coerr, Eleanor, *Sadako and the Thousand Paper Cranes.* New York: The Putnam Publishing Group, 1977.

Klagsbrun, Francine, Ed., *Free to Be You and Me.* New York: McGraw-Hill Book Co., 1974.

Singer, Isaac Bashevis, *Why Noah Chose the Dove.* New York: Farrar, Straus & Giroux, Inc., 1974.

Walker, Mary Lu, *Mary Lu Walker's Songs for Young Children*, Ramsey, N.J.: Paulist Press, 1973.

Walker, Mary Lu, *Peaceable Kingdom.* Joral Records, 1978.

Yashima, Taro, *Crow Boy.* New York: The Viking Press, 1955.

Organizations

• U.S. Committee for UNICEF, 331 East 38th Street, New York, NY 10016.
• CROP, Box 968, Elkhart, IN 46514.

Session 1

Affirmation: The Put-Up

Purpose

- To provide opportunities for children to experience affirmation (put-ups). The experience will include practicing affirmation of others, putting-up others rather than putting them down.

Background for Leader(s)

In today's culture there are many opportunities to experience the put-down. Little children are constantly being reminded that they are too little to do something or too big to cry. They are often told that they must wait until they are older before they can own certain toys or do certain things. Sometimes the put-down occurs when children encounter the competition of Little League sports. Programs such as ballet, gymnastics, and even "little miss" beauty pageants promote competitiveness among children.

In Session 3 we will look further at the adverse effects of competition. The point to be made now is that competition may be another put-down which damages a child's sense of self-worth.

The child who receives negative feedback as a steady diet will begin to show the results in his or her behavior. If a child is told he or she is naughty, the child will begin to live up to that reputation. If a child is called dumb or stupid, the child will think of himself or herself as dumb or stupid. What would happen if a new way of relating to one another were tried, so that instead of the put-down, a more affirming put-up were tried? The following activities have been designed to help children be affirmed even as they also affirm others.

Beginning Activities

"What Is the Shape of Your Name?" (15 minutes)

The supplies needed for this name tag activity are: a variety of colored construction paper, felt-tip markers, scissors, and straight pins or masking tape.

Have each person write or print his or her first name on a half sheet of construction paper. (Individuals may want to do this several times until satisfied with the shape their name makes.) Have each child outline the name with a felt-tip marker and look for any shape or design that emerges. (See illustration. It could turn into an animal, house, car, etc.)

Then have the children cut out the shapes and decorate them as desired. Pin or tape each child's name tag on him or her.

As participants complete their tags, invite each to share with one other person the design and any significance it may have for him or her. Suggest that the pairs introduce each other to the group, going around the circle until all have been presented. Leaders might want to model the type of response that is desired. "This is Betty, and her name shape is a kitty. She loves cats."

Music for Affirmation (10 minutes)

Sing together familiar songs, such as "If You're Happy and You Know It" and "There Is a Whole World in God's Hands" (similar to "He's Got the Whole World in His Hands.")

Begin to teach the theme song for this unit, "Happy Are Those Who Make Peace." Later on in the unit you will be able to sing the song as a round and to add new words to it.

To the tune of "Twinkle Twinkle Little Star," you can create a song tailored to the points you want to emphasize. For example:

Here are things that make for peace;
Sharing makes joy to increase.
Peace may start from honest praise.
Put-ups are some simple ways.
Here are things that make for peace;
Sharing makes joy to increase.

Read Romans 14:19a and explain that the songs you will be singing for the next few sessions will be based on things that help us make and keep peace. Perhaps the children will suggest appropriate songs or set the Bible verse to music, either during the sessions or while they are at home practicing on an instrument or listening to music.

25

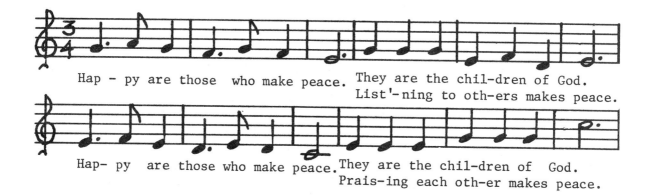

Hap - py are those who make peace. They are the chil-dren of God.
List'-ning to oth-ers makes peace.

Hap - py are those who make peace. They are the chil-dren of God.
Prais-ing each oth-er makes peace.

Gwendolyn Miller, "Happy Are Those Who Make Peace," *Let's Be Friends* (Elgin, Illinois: Brethren Press, 1971), p. 30. Copyright 1971, Church of the Brethren General Board. Used by permission. Words are adapted.

Developing Activities

Storytelling (10 minutes)

Crow Boy, by Taro Yashima is a modern story with illustrations. It is available in most public libraries. If you cannot obtain it, plan to tell a lively story based on the following condensed version.

Crow Boy is the story of a strange little boy who was ignored and put down by his classmates, who called him Tiny Boy. Through the understanding of his teacher the boy's talents were recognized. His nickname was changed to Crow Boy after the class talent show, when he gave wonderful imitations of crows. All the children came to appreciate the gifts of the boy and he became Crow Boy, loved by all.

Discussion (10 minutes)

Supplies needed for this activity are: newsprint and marker.

Help children think about put-downs. Working together as a group, list the ways Crow Boy was put down in the story. The leader may record on newsprint the responses. Ask the group members "Have you experienced any of the kinds of put-downs that Crow Boy experienced? Then ask the group about other kinds of put-downs which they have seen or heard. Add these to the list.

Define put-ups. Put-ups are the opposite of put-downs. Anything that can make people feel good about themselves is called a put-up. The put-up says something good about another person. List on newsprint ways Crow Boy was affirmed or put up. List ways group members have experienced the put-up.

Self-Affirming Activities

Invite children to select one of the following learning centers.

Designing a T-Shirt Slogan *(30 minutes)*

This exercise encourages children to think about themselves and what they like to do. Draw a picture of a T-shirt on a sheet of paper. Make enough copies of this picture so that each participant may have at least one T-shirt picture.

Instruct the children about how to make the T-shirt slogan with the following directions: You have a picture of a T-shirt. Pretend you are creating a slogan for your personal T-shirt. Write or print your name on the shirt, using a style you like. Then draw a picture of something you like to do. Then write one word which describes you. This word may or may not relate to the picture.

When children have completed their slogans, encourage them to share these with one another. This T-shirt activity might be expanded into a project in which children transfer their work onto a real shirt.

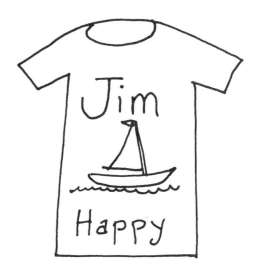

Baking Initial Pretzels

In this activity children will make and bake pretzels in the shapes of their initials or names, using the following recipe and instructions. Preheat oven: 425°

Dough for 20 pretzels:
  1 1/2 cup (375 ml) lukewarm water
  1 package dry yeast
  4 cups (1000 ml) flour
  1 tablespoon (15 ml) sugar
  1 teaspoon (5 ml) salt
  1 egg, slightly beaten with 1 teaspoon (5 ml) water
  (save mixture to paint pretzels with brush)
  Kosher salt

In large bowl, mix 1 1/2 cup (375 ml) lukewarm water and yeast. Combine 3 cups (750 ml) flour and sugar and salt. Add flour mixture to yeast mixture. Knead mixture on counter, adding remaining cup of flour. Divide dough into 20 parts, giving each child a portion. Suggest that the children knead their portion and then form it into their initials or name. Place dough initials on greased pan. Paint completed initials with the egg/water mixture. Sprinkle pretzels with kosher salt. Bake the pretzels until they are golden, about 20 minutes. Pretzels will be soft and chewy.

Note: Children should be involved in clean-up after art and cooking projects.

Closing Activities

Game: People to People (10 minutes)

This game can be played indoors or outside. Ask the children to pair up and stand in a circle, facing the leader, who is in the center of the circle. The leader sets a beat by clapping or snapping his or her fingers and chanting "people to people." Everyone claps in rhythm. Next the leader calls a body part, keeping the same rhythm. The leader may say: "back to back," and the partners assume the position. The leader continues suggesting positions: "hip to hip," "knee to knee." Partners continue motions until leader shouts "people to people." That's the signal for everyone to scamper about and find a new partner. The leader finds a partner too, and the new person without a partner becomes the new leader.

From Andrew Fluegelman, *More New Games* (New York: Doubleday and Co., Inc., 1981)

Worship (5 minutes)

Print the following Scripture verse on newsprint: "See how much the Father has loved us! His love is so great that we are called God's children. . . ." (1 John 3:1a, TEV). Read this verse together. Then have a time of prayer. Invite the children to say sentence prayers for themselves and one another.

Bible Used in This Session: Romans 14:19a; 1 John 3:1a

Session 2

Communication: The Key to Peaceful Interaction

Purpose

- To enable children to practice communication skills.

Background for Leader(s)

How important is communication? T. Harrell Allen, speech professor at the University of Southern California, estimates that eighty-five out of every hundred couples who seek marriage counseling have failed in their efforts to communicate. If the husband and wife cannot communicate with one another, probably there will be little interaction with their children. Families without communication will at best be characterized by indifference but not by peaceful interaction. In the article which is mentioned in the Resource Section of this unit, Allen suggests that the most important step in communication is accepting all feelings. The listener learns to listen with the "inner ear," picking up emotions and feelings that the person is unable to express.

In 1 Corinthians 13:4-6, we read: "Love is patient and kind; love is not jealous or boastful; it is not arrogant or rude. Love does not insist on its own way; it is not irritable or resentful; it does not rejoice at wrong, but rejoices in the right."

The key to peaceful interaction is communication which grows from the communion of love. If we can use these ideas from the "love chapter," we can model good communication skills. Teachers model good communication when they practice patience and kindness, accept feelings from group members, and rejoice in the good things in which pupils are involved. The following exercises and activities are suggested as ways to help children learn appropriate ways of communicating with others.

Beginning Activities (30-40 minutes)

Communication of Feelings

Provide a wall display of photographs or magazine pictures of people displaying different emotions: happy, sad, fearful, angry, etc. Briefly indicate how different facial expressions communicate different feelings.

Collage of Feelings

Invite each member of the group to create individually a collage about feelings, using pictures selected from magazines. The materials you will need for the activity are: magazines, scissors, glue, and construction paper.

When the children have completed this activity, ask them to share their collages, and to relate experiences in which they have had some of the feelings pictured on their collages.

Music

Sing the unit theme song once and then try to sing it as a round. Read Matthew 5:9. If you use Today's English Version the children will more easily see the connection between the song and the Bible.

"Happy are those who work for peace;
God will call them his children!"

If you wish to include another music activity, then secure a copy of the recording "Free to Be You and Me" and possibly the book by the same title. Play the song from the album entitled "It's All Right to Cry." Talk about feelings the song brings out. Show the photographs which are included in the book. These show many people—men and women, young and old—in tears. Ask the group, "Is it all right for both boys and girls to cry?" After some discussion invite the group to sing the song. You may provide printed words on either a large chart or an overhead projector, or make a copy for each person.

Developing Activities (35 minutes)

Communication Exercises

Nonverbal Mirroring

The object of this exercise is for two people to communicate nonverbally, mirroring one another's motions and emotions. Ask the group to divide into pairs. One member of each pair will be A and the other B. Ask the A's to begin doing body motions and facial expressions and the Bs to copy those movements. After a few minutes, ask the Bs to be the leaders. Finally suggest that they change leadership as they wish. Talk in small groups about the experience. Was it easier to follow or to lead?

Following Directions

This is an exercise to improve listening skills. Ask for three volunteers who will be told to listen to a set of directions, which will be given only once. One volunteer at a time will perform the tasks as directed. The group will observe whether or not the three volunteers followed the directions. Be sure to let all three volunteers finish before asking for comments from the group. Make the directions fairly complicated but not too long. For example: "Go to the window, knock on the pane three times, clap your hands four times, turn around and return to your seat, then shake hands with the person on your left and cross your legs." The volunteers will have to listen carefully in order to follow the directions, and observers will have to listen and observe to know whether any mistakes were made.

Discuss the part that listening plays in understanding one another. Use such questions as: Who listens more, children or adults? Encourage the children to talk about times they have felt someone really listened to them.

I Love Ya, Honey, but I Just Can't Smile (Circle Game)

If time permits, use this game which requires participants to give attention and respond. Participants sit in a circle. Leader begins by saying to the person on his or her right, "Do you love me, honey?" The person responds, "Yes, I love ya, honey, but I just can't smile." The first person attempts to make the second person smile. If in three attempts, the person does not smile, go on to the next person. This continues around the circle until the leader is asked the question and is made to smile.

Closing Activity (5 minutes)

Write these words on newsprint or chalkboard:

Church
Communication
Community
Communion

Read the words aloud and challenge the group to think of ways that the words are similar. Younger children may mention similarities in spelling. More mature children may point out connections in meaning. The church is a community of people whose common faith is in Jesus. One expression of that faith is the service of Communion. As we consider peace, we need to remember all the things, including faith, which we have in common with other people. Perhaps our common faith could become a bridge for communication and for community among all people.

Ask the children to bring a piece of fruit to the next session. Create a little suspense by not telling what you will do with the fruit. Merely announce that it will have to do with the group as a community.

Close by praying the Lord's Prayer together.

> **Bible Used in This Session**: 1 Corinthians 13:4-6; Matthew 5:9

29

Session 3

Cooperation: When Everyone Wins

Purpose
- To provide experiences that involve children in co-operative ways rather than competition.

Background for Leader(s)

Competition is as American as apple pie. It is an important aspect of many other modern cultures, too. Everyone wants to be a winner; parents encourage their children to be first in their class and to be on the winning team in sports activities. It is natural to want one's child to be successful. However, our culture needs to look again at competition and its effects on all people, particularly children. Being a winner in some competitive activity does not necessarily enhance one's sense of self-worth, except in that activity. Being a loser detracts from self-worth, not only in that activity but in all of life. So, competition may adversely affect winners by inculcating a false sense of human worth; and may adversely affect losers by inculcating a sense of failure. When winning is everything, there is not much room for the underachiever, the poor athlete, the uncoordinated child.

In our churches we can model some cooperative ways of living and playing together that eliminate the competitiveness children encounter in other places. For example, the competitive game of volleyball can be changed to a cooperative, friendly game of blanketball, whereby teams gather around blankets and toss a ball from one blanket to another. A team effort of this kind enables everyone to play regardless of athletic skill. The material for this session is designed to provide fun and a sense of belonging and to promote cooperation.

Beginning Activities

Cooperative Musical Chairs (10 minutes)

Arrange chairs as for musical chairs, either back to back or in a circle. As in the traditional game, children march around the chairs as music is played. When the music stops, all participants sit. One by one the chairs are removed, but players remain in the game by simply sharing chairs or laps until only one chair remains with a pile of people sitting on one chair. (Guaranteed to be hilarious.)

Group Singing (10 minutes)

Sing the theme song for the unit as a round. When the children are confident in singing it, you may change the second line to "Diff'rent parts will make a whole."

The song "There's a Whole World in God's Hands" is appropriate for this session. Try the following variation and movements:

1. There's a whole world in God's hands
   (*Sing three times.*)
   (*Join hands and form a circle, moving in and out.*)
   Last Line: There's a whole world in God's hands.

2. There's a little bitty baby in God's hands
   (*Sing three times.*)
   (*Fold arms as if rocking a baby.*)
   Last line:
   There's a whole world in God's hands.

3. There's you and me, partner, in God's hands
   (*Sing three times.*)
   (*Every other person turns to the right and these two children become partners. They face each other and point to each other and then to themselves. If there is an odd number of children, the adult leader becomes a partner.*)
   Last line:
   There's a whole world in God's hands.

4. There's everybody here right in God's hands.
   (*Sing three times.*)
   (*Form the circle again; clasp hands and raise them high.*)
   Last Line:
   There's a whole world in God's hands.

Developing Activities

Put Your World Together (25 minutes)

Prepare some world puzzles before the session begins. Begin with enough circles so that you have one for every three or four children. Cut the circles (which represent worlds) into six to eight pieces. Make the cuts or pieces simple. You can cut several circles at once because you want each world to have the same parts. Example:

Clip together three or four pieces of each circle. Put them in separate envelopes. Put all of the other pieces into a pile and mix them up. Redistribute the mixed-up pieces at random and put three or four pieces in each envelope.

When the children arrive, divide them into as many groups as you have envelopes with world pieces. Explain that each group is entitled to·a world of its own, but somehow the worlds have come to pieces. Give each group an envelope with pieces of the world. In order to put their world together, they may give, trade, and cooperate, but they are not to talk. After 10 or 15 minutes, stop the process.

When all of the worlds have been completed, lead a discussion about their feelings during the exercise. Ask such questions as: Was anyone refused when he or she tried to get a piece from another group? How did it feel to have to go to another group and ask for something? How did it feel to be able to refuse or to trade or give? If one group finished before the others, did that group try to help another group, or what did they do? If no group finished, what prevented them? Did working without language help or hinder putting the world together? Did it make them want to grab? Did it make them more thoughtful?

Conclude the exercise by showing that all the worlds are really the same. Lay the identical pieces one on top of the other and make one world.

Cooperative Animals (20 minutes)

This is a cooperative art activity. The supplies you will need are: large (12 by 18 inches; 31 by 46 cm) pieces of construction paper, scissors, crayons, staplers, masking tape.

In groups of five or six, create cooperative animals. Each group member draws a different part of an imaginary animal.

Members may pick from a hat the names of the parts they will draw or decide cooperatively among themselves who will draw what part. Each group will assemble its animal using staples or tape. Asking members of one group to close their eyes while another group arranges its animal adds to the adventure. At the completion of the exercise ask group members to share what they like about the cooperative animals.

Call attention to how different parts contributed to the fantastic animals.

Closing Activities (20 minutes)

Cooperative Fruit Salad

Materials needed for this activity are: various kinds of fruit, salad dressing, knives for preparing the fruit, and eating utensils.

You may need to provide fruit in addition to whatever the children bring. Perhaps your contribution will include some type of fruit the children do not usually eat, such as lemons or olives. Or, you may include fruit which is especially popular in a different neighborhood or culture.

Invite children to create a salad, working together to produce a treat which is more delicious because of the interaction of its various parts.

Worship

Use 1 Corinthians 12:14-20 as a responsive reading. Choose a modern language version, if possible. You may want to copy the passage onto newsprint or a chalkboard if you do not have enough copies of the same version of the Bible.

Ask for a volunteer to read the even-numbered verses; in other words, to be the leader. Or, you may have several solo readers instead of only one, while the group reads in unison the odd-numbered verses. Finally, for emphasis, have everyone read together verse 20 after the solo reading.

Bible Used in This Session: 1 Corinthians 12:14-20

Session 4

Peaceful Conflict

Purpose

● To provide opportunities for children to think about peaceful ways to work through conflict situations.

Background for Leader(s)

Some of us grew up believing that all conflict is bad. We were made to feel guilty if we got into fights with sisters and brothers. And the fear of what the neighbors would think often kept us from following our aggressive tendencies. As a result we submerged our anger and never learned to deal with it in a constructive manner. Helping children deal with their problems and conflicts in constructive ways can teach important skills for living in today's world.

This session is planned to help children face conflict openly, to understand the human dimensions in conflict situations, and to learn peaceful ways of resolving conflicts.

Beginning Activities (10 minutes)

Conflict and the "One-Eyed Monster"

Using newsprint or chalkboard, ask children to list television programs or motion pictures in which conflict situations are seen. Talk about the programs or movies, discussing why the characters seem to be in conflict. If you have already used the unit on computers and video games, ask the children to recall and add to what was talked about in the session on violence (pages 16-18).

Conflict Situations Children Face

Ask children to list situations in their lives which cause conflict. Add these ideas to the newsprint chart. Discuss the problems children have listed.

Developing Activities

Role-Playing Conflict Situations (40 minutes)

Role-Play About a Decision

Joe and Julio are playing a game of catch. Andy comes along and asks to play too. Joe says "no," because he doesn't like Andy. Julio hesitates. The game does not have to be limited to only two players. (For this scene be sure to discuss how all the participants felt.)

Role Play About a Bully

In a school corridor, Sam the bully knocks the books out of Pat's arms. Then Sam steps on the books and laughs. (Pat may be either a girl or boy.)

Role Play About Friends

In the school lunchroom Sharon has two pieces of cake. She is eating one, and has just given the other piece to Linda, her best friend. Then Rosita comes along and would like some cake. Sharon doesn't particularly like Rosita, but Linda does like her.

Role Play About Possessions

In school Pam and Michelle are fighting over a pencil. Pam accuses Michelle of stealing the pencil. Michelle says she brought the pencil from home.

What About Conflict in the World?

After the role plays about conflict among individuals, lead into a discussion of conflict among nations. Point out the similarities in the two. Often it appears that nations act in ways similar to the way the characters acted in the role plays. For instance nations become exclusive, nations sometimes bully other nations, and nations fight over possessions. Often the causes of the conflicts are the result of misunderstandings.

Present the information that there are organizations working so that nations may understand one another and cooperate on projects to help people. One organization which the children will identify with is UNICEF. Talk about some of the things that UNICEF does to promote peace, such as the collection of money at Halloween which goes to buy food for hungry families.

Another organization is CROP. Children may have participated in CROP walks, which raise funds for farm and food projects in needy areas of the world.

Group Singing (15 minutes)

If you know it, "Frère Jacques" can be sung in several languages, accompanied by rhythm instruments. "Small World" also lends itself to rhythm instrument accompaniment.

Sing the unit theme song "Those Who Make Peace." Perhaps the children can add another stanza or two. They might suggest replacing "They Are the Children of God" with "Praising Each Other Makes Peace," or "List'ning to Others Makes Peace."

Closing Activities (25 minutes)

Pen Pal Letters

Provide notepaper, pencils, crayons, and envelopes for each member. Brainstorm some ideas to be included in a pen pal letter to a person in another country. Allow time for letter writing, helping the younger children with ideas for content. Suggest that the children tell a little about themselves and make a very simple statement about their reason for wanting a pen pal from another country. Children may want to add illustrations or decorations to their letters. The letters may be mailed to an agency such as the following:

Dear Pen Pal
P.O. Box 4054
Santa Barbara, CA 93103

Sharing Pax Cakes or Crackers

While the children are finishing their pen pal letters, get ready for sharing pax cakes (pancakes or crackers). You will need three pax cakes for each participant. Because the pax cakes may be rather dry, you may want to have water or juice for each person.

When you are ready to begin, tell the children that the group is going to have its own variation of the tradition of pax cakes. Explain to the children that *pax* is the Latin word for "peace." Long ago people who had quarreled during the past year met and ate pax cakes together. With the eating of each pax cake they asked for and received forgiveness from each other and from God.

Describe the procedure something like this: "Each time

I pass the plate of crackers (or pancakes), take only one. After I say a few words to help you recall about being forgiven, eat one of the crackers slowly while you think and pray. Let's not have any other talking until we have had three pax cakes."

Eating the Cakes or Crackers

Read Romans 14:19a and Mark 11:25.

First pax cake. Pass the cakes or crackers. Suggest: "As you eat your first pax cake, think of the family members you have quarreled with recently: mother, father, sisters, brothers. Forgive them. Ask God to forgive you for anything you did to cause the quarrel or keep it going."

Second pax cake. Pass the tray of crackers or pancakes again. "As you eat your second cake, think of friends or neighbors you may have quarreled with. Forgive them for anything mean they have done to you. Ask God for forgiveness for yourself."

Third pax cake. Pass the crackers or pancakes a third time. "As you eat your third cake, think of persons in this group you have quarreled with or have had a hard time getting along with. Forgive them silently. Ask God for forgiveness for anything that you have done to keep from being as friendly as you could be. Let us be thankful that God forgives us, God loves us. Amen."

Bible Used in This Session: Romans 14:19a, Mark 11:25

33

Session 5

Becoming Peacemakers

Purpose

● To provide activities through which children may learn and become committed to peacemaking.

Background for Leader(s)

Becoming peacemakers is not just a one-shot try; rather it requires continued commitment throughout one's life. We can begin the task of becoming peacemakers by affirming others and trying consciously not to put down ourselves and other people. We can work purposefully to communicate with other people, trying to practice patience and love in our dealings with others. Finally, we can seek for opportunities to cooperate with other people in noncompetitive ways of living and playing.

This final session of the unit will attempt to summarize the preceding four sessions and will focus on commitment to living peacefully in our world. What kinds of things can we do to help us become peacemakers now and for the rest of our lives?

Beginning Activities

Taking Stock of Our Toys (10 minutes)

Using newsprint or chalkboard, list popular or favorite toys owned by members of the group. How many of them have to do with war and conflict? Underline those toys listed that are "war toys." Next, list toys that don't have to do with competition and fighting. Discuss the value of toys that are noncompetitive. What are the merits of these kinds of toys? Suggest that children discuss with their parents any decisions they make concerning toy guns and other war toys.

If you have already used the unit, "Jesus in the Electronic Age," this discussion of toys related to war and violence may be a review. It may also bring new insights.

Music and Movement: Dance of Peace (20 minutes)

Using colored streamers or scarves, invite children to show through movement their feelings about a world of peace. They may think of the different colored streamers as representing different races of people. For background music, use a recording of "The Swan" from *The Carnival of Animals* by Saint-Saens, or a flowing hymn tune such as "We Would be Building," based on *Finlandia* by Jean Sibelius. Suggest that the children weave in and out, waving their streamers or scarves in a peaceful tapestry of movement in time to the music. Encourage dancers to interact nonverbally by waving their streamers together as they strive to express their feelings through movement.

Developing Activities (45 minutes)

Storytelling

Tell the story of *Sadako and the Thousand Paper Cranes* by Eleanor Coerr. A synopsis of this story follows:

This is a story based on the life of a real little girl, Sadako, who lived in Japan from 1943 to 1955. Sadako was in Hiroshima when the United States Air Force dropped an atom bomb on the city. Ten years later she died as a result of radiation from the bomb.

In the story, Sadako's friend Chizuko visits her in the hospital and brings Sadako a golden crane folded out of paper. Chizuko reminds Sadako that there was an old story that said the crane was believed to have lived one thousand years. The gods would grant the wish of anyone who could fold one thousand paper cranes. If Sadako can fold a thousand cranes, the gods will make her healthy again. Sadako determines to fold one thousand cranes. She is able to fold only 644 before she dies. Her classmates fold the remaining 356 cranes, so that one thousand paper cranes are buried with Sadako. A monument has been erected to Sadako in Hiroshima Peace Park. On the monument is a statue of Sadako, standing on a granite mountain. She is holding a golden crane in outstretched hands. Engraved on the base of the statue are these words:

> This is our cry,
> This is our prayer,
> Peace in the world.

Activities for Recall and Summarizing

Put Music to Words

Invite children to create a melody for the words on the statue of Sadako. When the tune is set, they may sing it for your congregation or put it on tape. The taped song can be used in different ways: for shut-ins, for sharing at home with family, or as a resource in a neighborhood day-care center.

Make Place Mats

Often children like to have something to take home at the end of a unit study. They may make simple place mats on which they draw a crane to remind them of Sadako and the brief poem about peace.

Use the pattern given in this book and have children cut out cranes from a variety of types of paper. Each child will also need a sheet of wax paper approximately 24 by 30 inches (61 by 77 cm).

Have children fold the wax paper in half with the cranes inside. With a warm, not hot, iron show the children how to press the wax paper ''sandwich'' so that the wax paper sticks together. When this is done, a place mat has been created.

Peace Bumper Stickers

The supplies needed for this activity are: solid-color contact paper and permanent magic markers. Children will choose a word or phrase that emphasizes how they feel about peace. After choosing the word or phrase, they plan the best way to letter their bumper sticker. They may wish to make more than one, taking an extra bumper sticker for bikes or wagons.

Peace Mobiles

Supplies for this activity include: cardboard, markers, string, and coat hangers. Children will brainstorm symbols of peace in order to make a mobile. Some ideas might include doves, rainbows, cranes, hearts, silhouettes of peo-

ple holding hands, and so forth. Anything that reminds the children of peace can become a symbol.

Closing Activities (15 minutes)

Sharing with One Another

Invite children to share their creations with the other children. Allow time for individuals to tell the group about their projects.

Create a Litany of Peace based on Matthew 5:9 (TEV)

''Happy are those who work for peace;
God will call them his children!''

Ask children to make statements of things they would like to do to be peacemakers. After each statement, repeat together the verse printed above from Matthew.

Singing

Sing the unit theme song. If your group created a song, sing it again now.

Passing the Peace

Close the session by passing the peace. One at a time have each child hold the hands of the person to his or her right and say, ''The peace of God be with you.'' After everyone has repeated the words, the leader may close with a simple ''Amen.''

Bible Used in This Session: Matthew 5:9

UNIT 3

Learning About the Bible

by Phyllis Heusser

Unit Introduction

Welcome to a quick trip through history! For many of us the word "history" brings back memories of dreary data, of facts, dates, and names to be learned. This trip through the history of our Bible is not to be drudgery, but we will experience the Bible through the daily lives of God's people.

Children see the Bible as a completed book, an accomplished fact. They have not seen it change in their lifetime, and may therefore assume that it was always as they know it. They think that it has been the same for their parents and grandparents as it is for them. The concept of the Bible as a developing entity may be entirely new to them.

The four sessions in this unit are designed to help children to understand this change by learning how the Bible came to us. This area of history has many facts and dates that are not included in this study. Our purpose here is to develop an overview of how the Bible has developed, to explore the Bible's organization in relation to its chronological development, to identify some of the historical settings in which the Bible came into existence, and to discover some of the major translations.

Session 1: "Which Came First?"

In this session the chronological development of the Bible is explored. This includes a brief look at the history of written communication. We begin a time line, to which we will add in each of the four sessions. The purpose of the time line is to give a sense of continuity and to relate the biblical and historical events to the development of the Bible. The actual dates on the time line are secondary to the sense of time and continuity.

Picture writing with clay and making scrolls will help the children realize how much more difficult it was long ago to preserve the written word than it is today. These activities help set the historical atmosphere for the children.

The progression from the story told around the campfire to the clay tablet writing to the scrolls is to give a sense of the progression of history. Though no portions of the Bible have been found on stone, we know that this was the first step in written language, and many of the peoples living near the Hebrews wrote their laws and records on stone tablets.

Session 2: From Jerusalem to Germany

At the beginning of this session, the children briefly experience what learning was like in the ancient synagogue school. Here learning was by rote. However, another kind of learning took place in the home. Here the Passover was reenacted yearly by the entire family. Through participation in this drama Jewish children then and now come to know part of their history in detail. They gain insight and understanding. Their history becomes a part of them.

We use drama to present the stories of Jerome, John Wycliffe, and William Tyndale. Through developing and enacting these dramas, the children will come to have some understanding of the times and people of these stories. They will have some understanding of how they felt about the Bible. The drama is not intended to be a performance as such, but a learning experience.

Making illuminated pages is an extension of the dramatic activity. The children can easily imagine how dreary it could be to copy page after page, day after day. They can understand and feel the desire to brighten things up a bit.

Session 3: From Germany to Us

The children begin by making a mural to review and reinforce the material covered in the first two sessions. Murals from ancient times have been discovered by archaeologists. They often show what life was like in those days. The discoveries of an old manuscript of the New Testament by Tischendorf and of the Dead Sea Scrolls by a shepherd boy have added to our store of knowledge about the Bible. Such stories are exciting to children, especially since the shepherd was a boy not much older than the children in your group when he made his discovery.

Archaeologists have uncovered clay dreidels (tops) from long ago. Playing a dreidel game that is centuries old helps the children to relate to daily life in Bible times.

Session 4: Learning Our Way Around in the Bible

Skills in using the Bible, such as finding verses easily, knowing what the different books are about, and knowing where to look for a given Scripture, or subject, are expected of Christians. Often it is assumed that memorizing the list of books of the Bible will develop those skills. However, children learn by doing. The best way for them to learn to use the Bible is to have lots of experiences in which they do use the Bible. Memorizing the books of the Bible by rote may only give them a string of names to recite. These names have more meaning when they are associated with the content of the book, its period of history, and its place in the organization of the Bible. These are learned by repeated use of the Bible. In this one session children will not be able to become skillful in the use of the Bible. However, their skill level will increase a bit, and it is hoped that they will begin to sense the organization of the Bible and feel more comfortable using it.

Materials to Have Ready

You probably have in your teaching area Bibles, pencils, crayons, paper, scissors. In addition you may want to gather the following items:

Session 1
- long strip of paper
- make-believe camp fire
- dowel sticks or substitute
- clay which hardens

Session 2
- map of New Testament churches (see page 42)
- erasable bond typing paper
- pens which must be dipped in ink
- ink

Session 3
- 3-by-5 cards (7.6 by 12.7 cm)
- paper for mural
- several different English language translations of the Bible
- ''counters'' for dreidel game
- light cardboard

Session 4
- names of books of Bible on individual 3-by-5 cards (7.6 by 12.7 cm)
- materials for mobile

Other Helpful Resources

Barragar, Pam, *Spiritual Growth Through Creative Drama.* Valley Forge: Judson Press, 1981.

Furnish, Dorothy J., *Exploring the Bible with Children.* Nashville: Abingdon Press, 1975.

Furnish, Dorothy J., *Living the Bible with Children.* Nashville: Abingdon Press, 1979.

Session 1

Which Came First?

Purpose

- To explore the chronological development of our present biblical content.

Background for Leader(s)

There are many dates and facts associated with the chronological development of the Bible, far more than we wish to include in this session. The important point in this trip through time is for the children to get a sense of the sequence of the development of the Bible and of the importance of God's communicating with people throughout history. The printed Bible as we know it is a recent development in that line of communication.

During this session the children will begin to develop a time line to help them get a sense of the distance between events. For this reason it is fairly important that the time line be as long as possible. If they can walk the time line, or stand along it to represent different events, they can better understand the length of time involved.

Storytelling has been a part of the Christian heritage from the beginning, being rooted in Hebrew tradition. In this session, the time around a simulated campfire is an example of the oral tradition, with the story as the focus. The story should be told well, so that it captures the interest of the children. If you feel you cannot tell the story the way you would like, you may want to invite a guest storyteller. This is in keeping with the storytelling tradition, for throughout history there have been those who told stories especially well, in exciting ways. These storytellers often traveled from group to group to pass on the heritage of the people through stories.

Beginning Activities

Begin a Time Line (5-10 minutes)

As the children arrive, have each write his or her name and birthdate, including the year, on a name tag. Have the children line up by birthdate. Place yourself at the end of the line, with some space between you and the oldest child. Explain that there are some years between the time that you were born and the time the oldest child was born. Explain that you have just made a line representing ____years (your age minus the age of the youngest child). Attach a strip of paper the length of the room to the wall. At the left end, label it "2000 B.C., Abraham." Explain the meaning of B.C. as "before Christ." At the center of the strip of paper, write "Jesus." At the far right, write the date of this year, A.D. 19__, and have each child in the group sign her or his name. Explain the meaning of A.D. It comes from the Latin *Anno Domini*, meaning "in the year of our Lord." You now have a time line with two thousand years before Christ and 19__ years after the time of Jesus, totaling almost four thousand years.

Developing Activities

Discussion and Story (15-20 minutes)

Have the children sit on the floor around a simulated campfire. You can pretend, or arrange a circle of stones and some sticks to look like a fire. A more realistic "fire" can be made by having a flashlight covered with red cellophane or tissue paper hidden in the wood. If the room is fairly dark, this will make a good campfire. Perhaps moving the group to a darkened room would help children to separate from the present and put themselves in the past.

Talk about what life might have been like two thousand years before Christ, with no TV, no radio, no electric lights. Ask what people might have done for entertainment in the evenings. Storytelling will probably be mentioned. Tell of the oral tradition, of storytellers preserving the traditions and history of the people.

Try an example of passing on a story by playing a game of "Gossip," also called "Telephone." Whisper a sentence to the child next to you, and have him or her pass it on. Send the message by whisper from one person to the next all the way around the circle. Have the last person repeat

2,000 B.C.   Jesus   A.D. 19__
Abraham

what she or he heard. Is the message the same one that started? Probably not. How then, were the stories preserved over hundreds of years without mistakes? Suggest that the people heard the stories over and over again and knew them very well. The stories were important to them, because they were the means of preserving the history of the people.

The children will need Bibles for the next part of this session. Have them available for them when they return from the ''fire.''

One of the most important stories of the history of God's people is that of the Exodus. The Exodus is the name for the journey the Israelites took out of Egypt from slavery. The first part of our Bible to be written down was from this time of wandering in the desert. It is called ''The Song of the Well.'' Look it up with the children in Numbers 21:17-18. Have those who find it quickly help any others who want some help. Discuss the importance of water to the people while they were in the desert. Read the verses with the children. How do they think the people felt about this well? What kinds of feelings do they get from these verses? Explain that the earliest record of this well was written about 2000 B.C., though the Exodus event took place about 1400 B.C. Add ''Exodus, 1400 B.C.'' and ''Song of the Well, first written Scripture, 1200 B.C.'' to the time line.

Briefly discuss how things were first recorded in writing. Be sure to let the children know that the oral tradition continued, but that other means of preserving information were also used. The first writings were on stone. Discuss how one might write on stone. Some possibilities are to chisel figures, to paint, to write with charcoal. Another way is to make impressions on clay and let it harden into stone. Later people learned to write on animal skins, and eventually they sewed the skins together and rolled them up. This was the beginning of scrolls.

As you mention dates and names ask different children to add them to your time line.

Many parts of the Old Testament were written down by different people in different places and at different times. Scholars believe that the book of Amos was the first of the prophetic writings to be written down, about 750 B.C. Also parts of the Bible were accepted as holy, as the word of God, at different times. We know that about 620 B.C., part of Deuteronomy was accepted by the people of Israel as the special word of God. We read about this in 2 Kings 22:3–23:3. This passage tells the story of King Josiah and the finding of the law. Help the children to locate the passage, but do not expect them to read it all. Instead, share this story with the children.

Josiah had been king of Judah for eighteen years when he made a big change in his rule. In 620 B.C. he discovered that for many years all the people had been giving money to the keepers of the temple. Josiah decided to use this money to repair the temple. He hired carpenters and builders and masons. The money was used by them to buy timber and stones to repair the temple. While the temple was being repaired, many things inside the temple were moved around and rearranged. In cleaning out an unused room, Hilkiah the high priest discovered a scroll. The scroll contained part of the book of Deuteronomy, telling of God's law. The priest gave the scroll to Shaphan, the secretary of the king. Shaphan reported to the king on the progress of the repairs and told him about the scroll that had been found. King Josiah asked Shaphan to read the scroll to him.

When the king heard the words of the scroll, he was so upset that he tore his clothes in anguish. He commanded Hilkiah and Shaphan, saying, ''Go, ask of the Lord for me and for the people and for all our land, about the words of this scroll that has been found. God must be very angry with us, for our people have not obeyed the words of this scroll for many years.''

So Hilkiah the priest and Shaphan the secretary went to Huldah the prophet and talked with her. She said to them, ''This is what God says. Tell the man who sent you, 'I am angry because the people have not kept the words of the scroll which the king of Judah read. The people have forsaken me and worshiped other gods, and I am angry. But I have seen that the king is very sorry. Therefore, he will not see the evil things that will happen.''' And they brought the message back to the king.

The king gathered all the elders and rulers and all the people of the land. He read all the words of the scroll of the covenant which had been found in the house of the Lord. And the king made a covenant before God. He promised to keep the commandments, and all the people joined the king in the covenant.

To keep this covenant the king commanded the priests and Huldah to destroy all those things that had been used in the worship of false gods, and to destroy all the places used for worship of false gods. Then the king commanded the people to keep the Passover as was written in the scroll, for such a remembrance had not been kept since the days of the Judges. As Josiah and the people made a covenant with God, they accepted the words of the scroll as holy, as the word of God to them. The words of the scroll are part of the book of Deuteronomy.

In Nehemiah 8:1–9:38, we read of the law being accepted as the word of God. After children locate the passage, share this summary of it.

Ezra, the priest, read and explained the laws to the people. They then worshiped God and asked God to forgive them for all the times they had not kept the laws. Ezra reminded the people of all God had done for them, retelling the story of the Exodus and of God bringing them to the Promised Land. Then he said, ''Because of all this, we make a firm covenant and write it, and our princes, our Levites, and our priests set their seal to it.'' This meant that all the people and their religious leaders accepted the law, or the first five books of our Bible, as the word of God.

This description was probably written about 365-350 B.C. In 200 B.C., the writings of the prophets were also accepted as holy. At the time of Jesus, the Scriptures included the law and the prophets. The other parts of our Old Testament, the writings and poetry, were known and used in worship and for instruction, but were not yet accepted as Scripture. For example, the Psalms were songs used in worship. The books of the Old Testament as we know it today were finally accepted in A.D. 90 by agreement of a group of bishops. They agreed that these books were useful to those who wanted to live as God wanted. This process of accepting and setting apart certain writings is called ''canonization.''

The New Testament has a similar history. The stories of Jesus were transmitted by oral tradition between the death of Jesus and A.D. 50. The first parts of the New Testament to be written were the letters of Paul, between A.D. 50 and 63. Between A.D. 70 and 100 the Gospels and Acts were written. The other letters and Revelation followed between A.D. 65 and 150. The accepted list of books in the New Testament as we know it (called the New Testament canon) was first listed in A.D. 367 by the Bishop of Alexandria, Athanasius. It was then widely accepted as God's Word.

After you have completed all the above explanations, review the items on the time line.

Make the Clay Tablets (20-25 minutes)

For this activity you will need clay which hardens. Here is a recipe: Mix equal parts of sawdust, wallpaper paste, and water. If the mixture is sticky, add more sawdust. Add a drop or two of oil of wintergreen or peppermint to cover the odor of the other ingredients. Store the clay in a plastic bag in a cool place. This material dries slowly when exposed to air. The clay can be painted with either acrylic or tempera paints after it is dry. Tempera works well with a little liquid starch added.

Prepare an area for work with clay by covering the tables with plastic. Have some dowels or rolling pins available for rolling the clay. Allow some time for the children to get used to the feel of the clay and to enjoy making shapes. Then guide them into rolling the clay into tablets. Have some instruments such as unsharpened pencils, chopsticks, or popsicle sticks for the children to use to make picture writing in the clay. You might suggest that they try to illustrate stories being transmitted by oral tradition, or Josiah's response to the discovery of the scroll, inventing their own picture writing. When the tablets are completed, let them dry.

Making Scrolls (15-20 minutes)

You will need a strip of paper 6 by 18 inches (about 15 by 46 cm) long and two dowels 8 inches (20 cm) long for each child. If you do not have sticks, use drinking straws or new pencils. Using tape, attach a dowel to each end of the strip of paper. Roll the two dowels toward the center of the paper.

Suggest that the children write a particular verse, such as Psalm 119:105, on their scrolls:

''Thy word is a lamp to my feet and a light to my path'' (RSV).

''Your word is a lamp to guide me and a light for my path'' (TEV).

If you have access to a Hebrew Bible, you could show the children what the verse looks like in Hebrew. Some of the children might like to try to copy from the Hebrew onto their scrolls.

Closing Activity (5 minutes)

Walk the length of the time line with the group. Briefly review the development of the Bible as you walk along. Close the session with a prayer of thanks for the Bible.

Bible Used in This Session: Numbers 21:17-18; 2 Kings 22:3–23:3; Nehemiah 8:1–9:38; Psalm 119:105

Session 2

From Jerusalem to Germany

Purpose

- To trace briefly and quickly the development of the Bible from Jerusalem to Germany.

Background for Leader(s)

The history of the Bible is a thrilling and exciting adventure. Our hope is that the children will catch some of that spirit through the activities of this session. Through the story of how the Bible has come to us, the children can see that God is still at work in the world, is still speaking as the Word is spread. The examples of Jerome, Wycliffe, and Tyndale not only show us that people have sacrificed even their lives so that we can have God's Word in our own language, but also that the responsibility for spreading the Word still must be accepted by Christians.

Beginning Activity

Set the Stage (10 minutes)

Have the children sit cross-legged on the floor. Explain that this is how they would have sat if they had been in Hebrew school at the time of Jesus. Ask what else they think would be different about school then and now. There were no books or papers or pencils. Only the teacher had a scroll. There were no electric lights, no movies, no computers, no pictures, and no recess. Girls did not go to school, but learned from their mothers at home. Students learned by repeating things together after their teacher. Try this with the Great Commission, Matthew 28:19-20. Say one phrase at a time and ask the children to repeat it after you. Do this several times, each time making the phrases longer, until the children can say the verses without your help. Ask the children whether or not they would like to learn in this way.

Share with the children that when Jesus was a boy, he spoke Aramaic although most of the Old Testament was written in Hebrew and Jesus would have learned it in that language. When the New Testament was written, the common language was Greek, so the New Testament was written in Greek.

Recall from the last session that the first books of the New Testament to be written were the letters of Paul. Paul was a missionary who took the Word of God to several cities around the Mediterranean. Find some of these cities on a map. Point out that Philippians was written to a church at Philippi, Corinthians to a church at Corinth, Romans to

a church at Rome, and so on. Share that many Christians took the Great Commission seriously, and went throughout the world to tell others of Jesus. As they did so, they told people who spoke many different languages. These people continued to tell others, so the oral tradition was used again to spread the word of God. The Bible, which was finally put together to include both the Old and New Testaments in A.D. 397, was still in Hebrew and Greek. Many people could not read or understand either language.

Developing Activities

Create Group Dramas (15-20 minutes)

Divide the class into three groups. Arrange for each group to include older as well as younger children. Make copies of each of the following stories and give each group one. Have them develop a skit or drama from the story to present to the rest of the class. As the groups are working, circulate among them and offer as much help as needed. Encourage them to develop dialogue.

If you decide to keep all the children in one group, use the story about Tyndale.

The Story of Jerome

The Old Testament had been written in Hebrew and the New Testament in Greek. By A.D. 382 many Christians could no longer read or speak these languages. Latin was a more common language. Several people had tried to translate the Scriptures into Latin, but had not been very successful.

A monk named Jerome lived in Rome at this time. He was a scholar, a person who loved to study and was always trying to learn things. He was the best Bible scholar of his day, and he knew Greek very well. A bishop of the church asked Jerome to make a translation of the Bible into Latin, so the people could read it in their own language.

Jerome began with the New Testament. He already knew the Greek language, and was able to make a beautiful translation of the New Testament into Latin.

The Old Testament Hebrew was more difficult. Jerome went to Palestine to study with some Hebrew rabbis so that he could translate the Old Testament from the oldest known scrolls.

Jerome finally finished his translation in A.D. 405. It took him over twenty years of study and hard work to make a translation of the Bible into Latin. Jerome's translation is called the Vulgate, which means the "translation of the common people." It was used by Christians for fifteen hundred years!

The Story of John Wycliffe

During the 1300s, John Wycliffe was a monk in England. He went into the countryside to the small villages and visited the churches. He discovered that the ministers in these churches did little to help the people understand the Bible. They conducted worship services in Latin, a language which the people, and many of the ministers themselves, did not understand.

Wycliffe wanted to translate the Bible into English so that the people could understand what God had to say to them. He spoke to many of his friends who were also monks. Some agreed to help him.

The church officials, however, did not want Wycliffe to make an English translation. They were angry because Wycliffe said that they were not the authority about God, but the Bible was.

Even though the church officials objected, Wycliffe and his friends went ahead and translated the Bible from Jerome's Latin Vulgate into English. They finished in 1380. The head of the church in England was so angry that he sentenced Wycliffe to life in prison. Wycliffe was imprisoned, but later released.

After Wycliffe died in 1384, the church officials dug up his bones, burned them, and scattered the ashes in a river. They hated him so much that they tried to wipe out any memory of him.

The Story of William Tyndale

William Tyndale felt that the English people should be able to read the Bible in their own language. In the early 1500s, he went to the English church authorities to ask permission to translate the Bible into English. They forbade him to do it. Nevertheless, Tyndale began translating the New Testament from Greek into English against the wishes of the church authorities. Tyndale heard that the printing press had been invented in Germany in 1450, so he went to Germany. He finished his New Testament translation and had three thousand copies printed. He knew that the church authorities would not allow him to bring them into England, so he and a friend smuggled them in. Tyndale's friend, Monmouth, was a shipper. He hid the copies of the New Testament in sacks of grain and bolts of cloth to bring them into England. Whenever copies of the New Testament were found by the church authorities, they would be burned. Tyndale and Monmouth continued to have them printed in Germany and smuggled into England.

Tyndale began to translate the Old Testament from Hebrew. During this time he was arrested and put into prison. His friends, including Monmouth, were also arrested, and some of them were burned at the stake. Tyndale was in prison for sixteen months. During that time he was allowed to have books brought to him. He continued to work on the translation of the Old Testament while he was in prison. His friends took sections of the translation out in the books they brought to him and which he returned. In 1536, Tyndale was sentenced to death for translating the Bible.

Presentation of Dramas (15-20 minutes)

Have each group share their drama with the class. When all are finished, discuss the sacrifice that some people have made that we might have the Bible in our own language. Have each group add the main character of their drama to the time line.

Make Illuminated Script Pages (15-20 minutes)

Tyndale had heard of the invention of the printing press in Germany in 1450. Before that time, all books had to be copied by hand. Bibles were copied by men called monks who spent their lives in monasteries copying page after page of the Bible. Sometimes they decorated these pages with designs around the borders and the first capital letter of a passage. Such decorated pages are called "illuminated pages." This not only made beautiful pages, but probably made their job a little less boring. If you have a Bible with an illuminated page, show it to the children.

Use erasable bond typing paper and pen and ink to make illuminated pages. If possible, use pens which must be dipped into ink, rather than ballpoint or felt-tip pens. You might have the children place a sheet of lined paper under the typing paper to help them write more neatly. Using Matthew 28:19a, have the children first write it lightly in

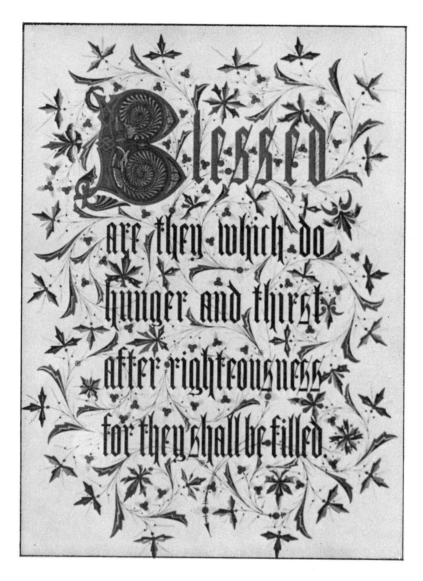

pencil. Then have them draw decorative designs around the edge of the paper and decorate the beginning letter of the verse. When they are satisfied with their designs, use pen and ink on the printing. Use colored felt-tip pens to "illuminate" the page. Many children have never used a pen that must be dipped in ink. This will not only be a new experience for them but will also be more realistic.

Paraphrase Scripture (10-15 minutes)

We have seen how some people have struggled and suffered to translate the Bible into languages that people can read and understand. Today we have the Bible in our own language. However, it is still sometimes difficult to understand. One way to help us understand what the Bible is saying to us is to put the meaning into our own words, to rephrase the Bible passage. This is called paraphrasing.

Read 2 Timothy 3:16 with the children in the Revised Standard or King James Version. Discuss what this Scripture means for them. You might want to have them look up some of the words in the dictionary, particularly "inspired," "reproof," and "righteousness." After your discussion, read the same verse from the J.B. Phillips translation.

"All Scripture is inspired by God and is useful
for teaching the faith and correcting error,
for re-setting the direction of a man's life
and training him in good living"
(2 Timothy 3:16, J.B. Phillips).

Discuss whether or not this translation is clearer for the children.

Have the children work in groups of three or four to make their own paraphrase of this passage.

Closing Activity (5 minutes)

Ask the children to share their paraphrases with the group.

Share with the children that during the next session, you will be looking at different versions and translations of the Bible. Ask them to bring any special Bibles that they might have to the next session.

Close with prayer.

> **Bible Used in This Session:** Matthew 28:19-20; 2 Timothy 3:16

Session 3

From Germany to Us

Purpose
- To continue briefly tracing the story of the Bible through several major translations.
- To explore some contributions from the scientific study of ancient times to our understanding of the development of the Bible.

Background for Leader(s)

There are many translations and versions of the Bible available today. Rather than seeing this as confusing, the children may come to recognize it as a natural progression, part of the tradition of wanting the Bible to be understood by all. It is important to note that some versions may be closer in meaning to the original sources than others, so it is helpful to know which were translated from the original Greek and Hebrew and which are paraphrases of other versions.

The role of archaeologists as detectives, discovering what the daily life of people in Bible times was like, can help us to discover some of the meaning of Scripture. Society in biblical times was very different from today, though some things remain constant. Children played games then and now. Even today, a top called the dreidel (drā'-dl) is part of the Hanukkah celebration for many Jewish children. Playing a game from long ago may help the children to see that, though the world may have been different, people are in many ways the same.

Beginning Activities

Display Bibles (5 minutes)

As children arrive, help them to arrange the Bibles they have brought. Have some 3-by-5-inch (7.7-by-12.8 cm) cards available so each child can write the name of the version of the Bible that he or she is sharing and the date it was first published. Help them to find the dates of publication on the title page or on the reverse of the title page. Encourage them to look through the different editions.

Make a Mural (20-25 minutes)

Briefly walk the time line with the children. As you walk, ask them what are the most important things that happened in the history of the Bible. Discuss how these events could be shown in pictures. Have each child select a scene he or she would like to draw as part of a mural. Provide a large sheet of butcher paper, long enough for all the children to work on. Arrange the children so that the events they are portraying will appear side by side in chronological order on the mural. They could draw the mural with paints and brushes, crayons, or colored markers.

Another way to do the mural would be to have children do pictures on separate sheets of paper and paste them to the one big mural paper.

Developing Activities

Sharing Together (15 minutes)

Briefly review by recalling the scenes of the mural. Recall that, during the last session, we heard of William Tyndale. As Tyndale was dying, he said, "Lord, open the eyes of the King of England." His prayer was answered, for, not long after Tyndale's death, King Henry VIII changed his mind. He ordered that each church have a copy of the Bible so that all who wanted could go to the church and read it for themselves. These Bibles were so large that they were called Great Bibles. They were chained to the church so no one could steal them.

During this same period, people in other countries were translating the Bible into their own languages. Martin Luther made a beautiful translation into German in the 1530s. As missionaries traveled about the world spreading the Good News, they translated the Bible into many languages. Today the Bible has been translated into over seventeen hundred languages and dialects.

Even though Tyndale's translation (completed by his friend, Miles Coverdale) was in English, it would be difficult for us to understand today. The English language has changed over the years. New translations become necessary as the language changes and as we make new discoveries about the ancient languages.

The Great Bibles in the churches of England were not all the same. They were different translations, and the people did not agree on which was best. So, in the early 1600s, King James ordered a new translation to be placed in all the churches. He had fifty-four scholars work together for more than three years. When the translation was completed, King James approved it. It was called the King James Authorized Version and was first printed in 1611.

Our language has changed since 1611. Also, very ancient copies of parts of the Bible have been found since the time of King James. These newly discovered manuscripts have been used to make more accurate translations. After many years of work, a group of Bible scholars working for the National Council of Churches here in the United States, published the Revised Standard Version (RSV) of the Bible in 1952. Another version you might use is the Good News Bible, also called Today's English Version (TEV). This was published by the American Bible Society in 1976.

Distribute a variety of versions among the children so that each has a Bible. Have each child share which translation he or she has. Have the children look up the following Scriptures in the various versions and compare them: Jeremiah 31:33, Matthew 5:14-16, 2 Timothy 2:15. Discuss which versions are easier to understand, which words are no longer part of our everyday language, and whether the meaning is the same in all versions. Be sure to have the children look at a King James Version, Revised Standard Version, Today's English Version, and any others that they may have brought.

Earlier it was said that new translations were made not only because language changed, but because more ancient manuscripts were found. People who study ancient artifacts and search for evidence of ancient civilizations are called archaeologists. Archaeologists tell us what life was like in other times. They study the buildings, the cities, and small items found from these ancient times. Sometimes such discoveries are made by people who are not archaeologists.

A German boy named Constantin Tischendorf was born in 1815. He became a paleographer, one who studies and translates ancient writings. Tischendorf felt that there must be more ancient manuscripts that had not been discovered. For years he hunted in monasteries and churches. He found very little of any importance. Then he heard of a monastery, the Convent of St. Catherine, that was supposed to be on the same spot where Moses had first written down the Ten Commandments. Tischendorf felt he must look there for ancient manuscripts. This monastery was high in the mountains of the Sinai Peninsula, and was very difficult to get to. It took days of traveling by camel across the desert. When he finally arrived, Tischendorf found that the monastery was surrounded by walls forty feet high. He could see no windows or doors. After a while, a chair was let down on ropes, and Tischendorf was pulled up the side of the wall into the monastery.

Inside the monastery, Tischendorf spent much time in the library, but he found nothing of interest. However, he unexpectedly made a discovery. One story has it that he saw a monk lighting a fire in a fireplace, using some old pieces of paper for kindling. Tischendorf could see that these papers were very old manuscripts, and he grabbed them from the fire. He saw that they were an ancient form of Greek. The monks allowed him to take 43 pages of these manuscripts, but they turned out to be of no great value. But he was sure that there were other manuscripts in the Convent of St. Catherine.

Tischendorf made two more trips to the monastery. On these occasions, he carried with him letters of introduction from the Czar of Russia, a person with some influence in that monastery. On the third trip, Tischendorf visited an old monk who also had an interest in old writings. He showed Tischendorf a carefully wrapped bundle. When it was unwrapped, Tischendorf saw that it was a manuscript of the New Testament made in the fourth century. He was very excited, but knew that the monks would not let him take it out of the monastery. After a long time, he got permission to take it to the Czar on a loan. It turned out that this manuscript was written in A.D. 325. Today it is in the British Museum in London, England, having been sold in 1933 by the Russians.

In 1947 another important discovery was made, this time by a shepherd boy. As the young man was watching his long-haired goats, he tossed a stone at one to get it to rejoin the flock. The stone flew into a cave on the mountain, and the shepherd heard the sound of breaking pottery. He climbed up to see what had made the sound. Inside the cave, he found several pottery jars. He was afraid, so he ran out of the cave.

Later he told a friend about the cave and the jars. They went back together to the cave and brought some of the jars back to camp. Inside the jars they found rolled-up strips of old leather with writing on them.

One day the boys took the leather strips into Jerusalem, and traded them to a shoemaker for a few coins. Sometime later, the cobbler looked at the old leather to see if it was good for repairing sandals. He noticed the writing on the strips of animal skin. He could not read, but knew that they must mean something. The cobbler was a Christian, so he took the pieces of leather to the priest in Jerusalem. The rolls of writing passed on in this manner from one person to another until they finally came to the attention of two American scholars who were studying in Jerusalem. They realized that these were very old manuscripts. Two of the scrolls turned out to be copies of the Book of Isaiah which were from about 290 B.C. The scholars compared these with later texts and found that, through the centuries, very few errors had been made by those who had copied the Scriptures by hand. These manuscripts are called the Dead Sea Scrolls, because the cave where they were found is near the Dead Sea.

Neither Tischendorf nor the shepherd boy was an archaeologist, but the discoveries of these two people have helped us learn more about our Bible. Archaeologists also have found many things which tell us what life was like in Bible times. Sometimes they find murals on walls that tell the history of a family or event in pictures. One of the things that archaeologists have found, and that is still being used today, is a toy called a dreidel. It is a kind of top used to play a game. Even today Jewish children play the dreidel game at Hanukkah, a Jewish holiday.

Make Dreidels (15-20 minutes)

The dreidel is a four-sided top, with a different symbol on each side. If you have a dreidel or can borrow one, you might bring it to show the children. Make dreidels by tracing on light cardboard the pattern found at the end of this session. Cut along the solid lines. Fold on the dashed lines, and glue or tape the sides together to form a cube. Push the sharpened end of a short pencil or a candy apple stick through the dreidel. Write the symbols on the four sides.

To play the game, players are each given an equal number of counters. These can be buttons, coins, or any other kind of markers. To start the game, players agree on the number of counters each is to put in the pot. Each player then spins the top in turn. If the top stops with 'Nun' (נ) on top, the player takes all the counters from the pot, and each player must again put in the agreed-upon number. If 'Gimel' (ג) is on top, the player takes half the counters in the pot. If 'Heh' (ה) is showing, the player gets nothing, and if 'Shin' (ש) is up, the player puts an extra counter in the pot. The game continues until each player has had an agreed-upon number of turns.

The four symbols on the dreidel stand for *Nes Gadol*

Hayak Sham, meaning "A great miracle occurred there." This refers to a great event in the history of the Hebrew people, when in 165 B.C. a lamp in the temple burned for eight days without oil being added. So the Hanukkah holiday is celebrated for eight days.

Closing Activity

Add to Time Line (5 minutes)

Add "King James Version, 1611," "Revised Standard Version, 1952," and "Today's English Version, 1976" to the time line.

During the next session, you will explore the organization of the Bible. Ask the children to bring their own Bibles with them.

Close with prayer.

Bible Used in This Session: Jeremiah 31:33; Matthew 5:14-16; 2 Timothy 2:15

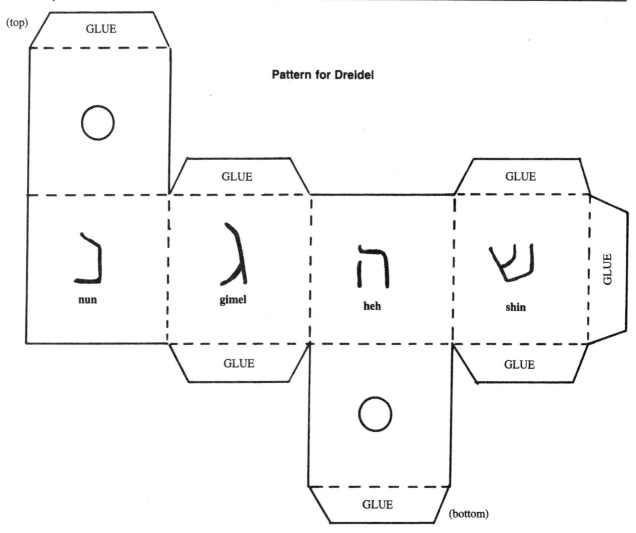

Pattern for Dreidel

(top) GLUE

GLUE GLUE GLUE

נ nun | ג gimel | ה heh | ש shin

GLUE GLUE

GLUE (bottom)

Session 4

Learning Our Way Around in the Bible

Purpose

- To explore and understand how the Bible is organized.
- To practice finding our way around in the Bible.

Background for Leader(s)

Our hope is that the children we teach will be using the Bible for the rest of their lives. If we can help them become familiar with its contents and to feel comfortable using it, we will be helping them to develop skills that will last a lifetime. Since there is a broad age span within your groups, there will also be a broad range of abilities and familiarity with the Bible. Encourage those who are more skilled to help the others when they need help. Encourage those who have beginning-level skills by giving them lots of sincere praise and affirmation. We want them to become excited about their developing skill with the Bible.

All the activities in this session are directed toward reinforcing knowledge of the organization of the Bible. The bookmarks, the mobiles, the twenty questions game, and looking up Scriptures will all build upon one another.

Beginning Activity

Make Bookmarks (10-15 minutes)

Have each child cut eight bookmarks from construction paper. These should be large enough so that children can copy words onto them. The children can decorate these by making the ends pointed, fringed, scalloped, or cut straight. Each bookmark is to be labeled with a section of the Bible. The sections are Law, History, Poetry, Prophets, Gospels, History, Letters, and Prophecy. Put these words where children can see them easily and copy them onto their bookmarks.

Developing Activities

Using the Bible (15 minutes)

Encourage the children to use their own Bibles for this activity. First, explore the Bible with them. Find the division between the Old and the New Testaments. Compare the sizes of these two sections. Relate these to the time line. The Old Testament concerns the B.C. times; and the New Testament concerns A.D. times. Find Genesis, Psalms, and Revelation. Point out the organization of the Bible into chapters and verses.

Help the children to place the markers in their Bibles. Find the beginning of each section, name the books in that section in order, pronouncing them clearly for the children, and tell what that section is about. There is a chart at the end of this session to help you.

At the first page of Genesis, have the children insert the marker labeled "Law." This section includes the first five books of the Bible: Genesis, Exodus, Leviticus, Numbers, and Deuteronomy. This section is also called "The books of Moses," "the Torah," or "the Pentateuch." In this section, we read of creation, the beginnings of the Hebrews as the children of God through Abraham, of Moses and the laws of God, and of the Promised Land.

The marker labeled "History" goes at the beginning of the book of Joshua. The history section includes twelve books, from Joshua through Esther. In these books we read the history of the Hebrew people from the time of Moses through the Exile and then about their return to rebuild Jerusalem. This is a period of about nine hundred years, from 1200 B.C. to 300 B.C. It includes the time of the Judges, and the kings of Israel and Judah, and the fall of both nations.

The Poetry section includes Job, Psalms, Proverbs, Ecclesiastes, and Song of Solomon (or Song of Songs). Job tells of the troubles that come to a good man, and how he maintains his faith in God. Psalms is the hymnal of Old Testament worship, including songs and prayers. Proverbs is a book of wise sayings. Ecclesiastes means "the preacher." It tells of God's wisdom as we see it in nature and in people. The Song of Solomon is a love poem.

The Old Testament Prophets section is a long and confusing section for children. There are many books with difficult names. It is helpful to point out that the first five, Isaiah, Jeremiah, Lamentations, Ezekiel, and Daniel are called "major prophets" because they are longer than the other books of prophecy. Mention that Lamentations is not a person's name, but means "sorrows" or "mourning." The remaining twelve books are referred to as minor prophets, and each is quite short. Go over the names as the children look at them in the table of contents, pronouncing them clearly. The prophets spoke for God, telling the people how God wanted them to live.

Place the marker labeled "Gospels" at the beginning of the New Testament. Matthew, Mark, Luke, and John will probably be quite familiar to the children. You might ask them to tell you what these books are about.

Acts is the only book of history in the New Testament. Share with the children that the complete name is "The Acts of the Apostles," and that this book tells of the early Christians and the beginning of the church.

The Letters is the longest and most difficult section of the New Testament. Explain that some of the books were written by Paul, and some were written by others. Those written by Paul are called Pauline epistles. Epistle is another word for letter. Some of the epistles are Romans, First and Second Corinthians, Galatians, Philippians, Colossians, First and Second Thessalonians, First and Second Timothy, Titus, and Philemon. All but the last four were written to churches. Refer to the map in Session 2 (page 42). Point out the cities where these churches were found. The authorship of some of the epistles is uncertain. The letters give advice on how to live according to God's will.

The prophecy section of the New Testament contains only one book, Revelation. It tells of John's vision in which the rule of God is finally triumphant over evil.

Help the children to review the organization by asking questions such as the following. "In which section of the Bible would I look to find parables or stories told by Jesus? Where would I find the Ten Commandments? Where would I find out what Paul thought about the church? In which section would I find the story of King David? Where would I find the people being reminded to love God? Which section tells about the early church? Where would I find poems about singing praises to God?"

Copy the following references onto newsprint or your chalkboard and have the children look them up.

Exodus 24:3	1 Samuel 12:6-8
Psalm 100	Jeremiah 1:4-5
Luke 4:16-20	Acts 6:7
Ephesians 1:1-2	Revelation 21:5-6

With each Scripture reference, tell them in which section of the Bible the verse is found. After reading each verse with the children or having a child read it, discuss how it is an example of that section.

This can be difficult for the children unless you keep things moving and encourage them in their search of the Scriptures. If they seem to be restless, go on to the next activity.

Play Bible Books Game (5-10 minutes)

Write the names of the books of the Bible, each on a separate 3-by-5-inch (7.7-by-12.8 cm) card. Pass out the cards at random to the children until all cards have been distributed. Briefly go over the books of the Bible by sections, naming the books in each section. Then call out a section, such as "Old Testament Law!" Each child who has a card labeled with a book in that section will stand and hold up the card. As the children get more familiar with the game, increase the pace. To end the game, have

the children return the cards to you in order. Have the child with Genesis hand the card to you and call out "Genesis!" Ask for the next book. After you have received Deuteronomy, indicate that you are moving on to the "Old Testament History" section. Move this along quickly, helping them to call out the next book whenever necessary.

Make Mobiles (15-20 minutes)

For each mobile you will need two pieces of lightweight cardboard or construction paper each 2½ by 9 inches (6.4 by 23.1 cm) and eight pieces each 1½ by 5 inches (3.8 by 12.8 cm). Label and hang the pieces as indicated in the illustration, using yarn or string. If you use construction paper, you can strengthen it by using gummed reinforcements over the holes or putting transparent tape over the paper before punching the holes. Have each child make a mobile to take home.

Play Twenty Questions (10-15 minutes)

Have a child, or two children working together, draw a card from the cards used in the Bible Books game. Have the other children see if they can guess which card was drawn by asking questions that can be answered "yes" or "no." Act as a resource for the player answering the questions and as game official, keeping track of the number of questions asked. If the group has not discovered the name of the book within twenty questions, have the answering child tell them, and have another child draw a card. Encourage the children to ask questions about which section of the Bible to narrow the choices, rather than just guessing the names of books. Play as long as there is interest in the game. You might suggest that the children keep their Bibles open to the table of contents so the names of the books are before them.

Closing Activities

Write Cinquain Poems (5-10 minutes)

Have the children work in twos or threes to write cinquain poems. Have each group choose a subject that is related to these sessions. Some suggested topics are Bible, Scripture, God, Christians. A cinquain is a five-line poem which does not have to rhyme. Cinquain follows this form. (Put this on newsprint or chalkboard.)

Line 1. One word, the title, a noun
Line 2. Two words, describing the title
Line 3. Three action words about the title
Line 4. Four words describing a feeling about the title
Line 5. One word that means the same as the title

Bible
God's Word
Helps us grow
We want to learn
Holy

Sharing Cinquains (5 minutes)

Share cinquains to express feelings about the Bible and our study of it. Close with prayer of thanks for the Bible and for the freedom and ability to use it.

Bible Used in This Session: Exodus 24:3; I Samuel 12:6-8; Psalm 100; Jeremiah 1:4-5; Luke 4:16-20; Acts 6:7; Ephesians 1:1-2; Revelation 21:5-6

LAW	HISTORY	POETRY	PROPHETS	GOSPELS	ACTS OF THE APOSTLES	LETTERS	PROPHECY
Genesis	Joshua	Job	Isaiah	Matthew	Acts	Romans	Revelation
Exodus	Judges	Psalms	Jeremiah	Mark		1 Corinthians	
Leviticus	Ruth	Proverbs	Lamentations	Luke		2 Corinthians	
Numbers	1 Samuel	Ecclesiastes	Ezekiel	John		Galatians	
Deuteronomy	2 Samuel	Song of Solomon	Daniel			Ephesians	
	1 Kings		Hosea			Philippians	
	2 Kings		Joel			Colossians	
	1 Chronicles		Amos			1 Thessalonians	
	2 Chronicles		Obadiah			2 Thessalonians	
	Ezra		Jonah			1 Timothy	
	Nehemiah		Micah			2 Timothy	
	Esther		Nahum			Titus	
			Habakkuk			Philemon	
			Zephaniah			Hebrews	
			Haggai			James	
			Zechariah			1 Peter	
			Malachi			2 Peter	
						1 John	
						2 John	
						3 John	
						Jude	

Children Face Life's Crises

by Marie Anderson

Unit Introduction

Change is inevitable in every child's life as he or she grows. Change can cause stress and crises in a child's world. The focus of this unit is to help children identify and deal constructively with some of the major changes in their lives.

The purpose of this unit is to help children see some of the changes or crises in their lives as positive rather than negative forces, i.e., as opportunities for making new friends, deepening other human relationships, and learning new skills.

A child may look happy on the outside but be full of stress, anxiety, and fear on the inside. "What stress can a child have?" you may ask. Some of us, as adults, are often filled with nostalgia when we remember our childhood as carefree, innocent, and happy. We often tend to treat children's pains

and problems as insignificant in comparison to our own. We need to learn not to see troubles as significant or insignificant, but to see the pain they produce. Because we believe the myth that "children are happy," and because children do not often articulate stress, we as adults do not often sense the fear trembling inside a child. We need to learn the language of a child's *behavior*.

Some of the behavioral signs of stress that would be pertinent for us as leaders to note are: general irritability, impulsiveness, inability to concentrate, loss of a sense of joy, fatigue, nervousness, stuttering, hyperactivity, anxiety, and fear. Stress can also evidence itself in physical symptoms such as aches and pains.

Stress comes from all sides. Whether the stress is based on facts or on feelings, the pain of it is real to the children caught in it. Children can become strong or weak because of a stressful situation or experience. How the adults in their lives influence them, especially during times of stress, can make the difference between whether they become strong or weak. Many life experiences are stressful to some degree. It is not possible, or even desirable, to eliminate all stressful life experiences from the lives of the children with whom we live and work. With the help of a supportive adult, children learn to cope with stress by moving through the anxiety they feel. The adult needs to provide physical, emotional, and spiritual support. I have tried to set up each of the five sessions in this unit so that you as leader can be that supportive adult. The sessions will help you to identify the crises involved and give children the opportunities to express their feelings freely and explore alternative ways of coping and dealing with the crises and their stresses. It is not safe to assume that children will outgrow their problems. It is wiser to be an active part of the process that will help to outgrow them. As positive experiences in dealing with stress accumulate, children develop the ability to see themselves as competent, strong, worthwhile individuals, and to see life as a challenge they can meet.

Erik Erikson, a noted psychiatrist, associates a large part of childhood stress with fear. He says children have eleven basic fears: withdrawal of support, suddenness, noise, being manipulated, interruption of vital activity, being deprived of a valuable possession, restraint, having no imposed controls, being exposed, remaining small, and being left alone. Some of these will be evident as you move through the sessions. Different children react differently to change and to new situations. One child may express fears openly; another may hide concerns under a show of eagerness to please. Children need reassurance and respect for their feelings.

Does this seem like a momentous task—helping children work through their crises? Well, it is, but we are not alone or without words of hope. Think of Psalm 40:1-3 (TEV) as key verses for this unit:

> I waited patiently for the Lord's help;
>   then he listened to me and heard my cry.
> He pulled me out of a dangerous pit,
>   out of the deadly quicksand.
> He set me safely on a rock
>   and made me secure.
> He taught me to sing a new song,
>   a song of praise to our God.
> Many who see this will take warning
>   and will put their trust in the Lord.

Please pray and take comfort in God's Word. As *you* put your trust in the Lord and "sing a new song" of praise, so will the children he calls you to lead.

Resources for the Unit

These books are available at your library, bookstore, or directly from the publishers, as listed.

1. *Ready-Set-Grow Series* by Joy Wilt. Word Inc., Educational Products Division, 4800 W. Waco Dr., Waco, Texas, 76796.
   a. *A Kid's Guide to Making Friends*
   b. *The Nitty-Gritty of Family Life*
   c. *Handling Your Ups and Downs*

2. Three books by Sara Bonnett Stein. 1983. Walker and Co., 720 Fifth Ave., New York, N.Y., 10019.
   a. *About Dying*
   b. *That New Baby*
   c. *On Divorce*

3. *Imagine That! Illustrated Poems and Creative Learning Experiences*, Joyce King and Carol Katzman. 1976. Scott, Foresman and Co., 1900 East Lake Ave., Glenview, Ill. 60025.

Session 1

Friendships Change

Purpose

- To help children become aware of their own friendship needs.
- To help children accept friendship changes, as a part of living.

Background for Leader(s)

To accept and learn how to deal positively with friendship changes is an important part of living. Dr. Keith Sehnert, in his book *Stress-Unstress* (Minneapolis: Augsburg Publishing House, 1981), states that twenty percent of American families move every year. That statistic means that the average family will move sometime within the next five years. Some children make friends and leave them as often as every two to three years. Ours is a mobile society. What does this fact mean for our children? Any time there is a move, a child must enter into new situations, and is forced to extend himself or herself to others and begin new relationships. Leaving their security behind, children are forced to enter a new neighborhood and a new school as well. Friendships in that environment have already been formed and they, the outsiders, have to find a place. Some are too withdrawn to try. Others attempt to prove themselves through outrageous behavior. Also, children must deal with leaving old friends behind. Although they may try to keep relationships alive through letters, phone calls, and promised visits, some friendships wilt and die. For some children, with the loss of friendship goes trust. Often when children balance the joy of friendship against the pain of separation, the pain overbalances and friendship loses out. Sometimes the child will even abandon the whole idea of friendship, for, although not having a friend hurts, losing a friend hurts even more. Note also that some of the children you will be working with may not have moved but may have lost a friend because the friend has moved. This loss often creates new situations and experiences that need to be dealt with also.

Moves, then, are seldom easy for children to handle. They cling to the known and comfortable and view with caution the unknown or strange. We need to encourage children to accept friendship changes as a part of living. We need to help them to be aware of their own friendship needs. As friendships change (for whatever reason), children need our encouragement to abandon their fears and apathy and to try to anticipate new friendships with joy and eagerness. New friendships can also soften a difficult experience and create a warm response to a new situation.

The Bible gives us positive examples of people who moved and from necessity developed new acquaintances and friendships. Joseph, for example, was wrenched from his family and homeland and forced to carve a niche for himself among strangers. His ability to establish positive friendships actually led to his opportunity for a position and influence in the land of Egypt and friendship with the most powerful ruler of the ancient world (see Genesis 37 and 39-50).

Children must face changes in life (moving, new schools, new interests etc.), and with these come the necessity and opportunity to develop new friends. Without the skills to initiate friendships, such changes can bring loneliness and alienation.

Before you begin with the children, it is important to remind yourself and them that everyone has a limited capacity for friendship and that each person has a different capacity for numbers of friendships. These capacities are neither good nor bad; they simply reflect the way God made our personalities and emotions. There is no special virtue in maintaining a large number of friends. The key is to love within our capacity and develop to the fullest those friendships that God gives us, knowing that friendships will ebb and flow in intensity and duration over time.

Beginning Activity

Friendship Survey (30 Minutes)

After welcoming each student, pass out the "Friendship Survey" (which you have duplicated from this book) and pencils. Each child needs one survey. Ask the children to hold them but not to read them just yet. At this point share a newsprint that looks something like the following:

A Friend Is Someone Who Likes You and Someone You Like. There Are Different Kinds of Friends:

1. *Acquaintances*
   —persons who like each other, but do not know each other very well
   —usually every person has many acquaintances

2. *Friends with whom we play or do things*
   —these friends see each other often
   —they like playing together or doing things together; going places together
   —usually every person has several people with whom to play or do things

3. *Best friends*
   —most best friends are close together and are able to see each other quite often (some are not)
   —but whether they are close or far apart, they love each other.

Share the definitions included on the newsprint with the children. After you have shared the definition of an acquaintance, allow the children to look at Question 1 on their surveys and write out the names of their acquaintances. You might open the topic by asking, "How many of you have acquaintances?" If they have none or very few, be sure to reassure them that that is OK. After the children have completed this question, review the second kind of friend and allow time for them to fill out their replies to Question 2. Perhaps you may want to introduce this question with another one, "How many of you have friends with whom you play or do things or go places?

The final category of friend is best friend. After you have reviewed the definition on the newsprint, allow time for the children to fill out answers to Question 3. Continue by allowing the children time to complete their replies to Questions 4 and 5.

After the children have finished the survey, continue by allowing them to share with the total group (if they feel comfortable doing so) different parts of their survey. Perhaps begin by asking someone to share what qualities they like in their best friends. After everyone has had a chance to

share, you might end the discussion by asking them to comment on question 5(e) of the survey. Ask "What does it take to have a friend?" Try to help the children identify their needs for friendship and how those needs are similar to, yet different from, the needs of other people.

Developing Activities

How Friendships Change—Dealing with Life-Size Friend #1 (20 minutes)

Draw two life-size outlines of a child. It would be helpful to have these prepared ahead of time. Cut out the drawings and mount both on the wall. Do not paint a face or clothing or any body details on these figures. Label them Friend #1 and Friend #2. On #1 attach two signs, "How Friendships Change" and "Feelings." (Save Friend #2 for later.)

Focusing on Friend #1, lead the children in a discussion of friendship changes. You may want to begin the discussion by saying something like this: "We've just talked about our need for friends and how important they are to us. But sometimes things happen to our friendships, and they change. How many of you have ever moved?" Allow the children time to respond and share their experiences and thoughts. Continue by saying something like this: "Moving from one house to another, one school to another, one church to another can cause our friendships to change, can't they? Let's put that idea down on our friend here." (Write the word "moving" on Friend #1 with a felt-tip pen.) Continue by asking the children how they felt about leaving a friend (or perhaps having a friend leave them by moving away). You might ask, "Were you sad? Lonely? What did you do? Did anyone help you?" Allow time for the children to discuss and share their feelings. You may receive such responses as "sad," "scared," "lonely," "mad," "mixed up," etc. Write their responses on Friend #1 under the heading "Feelings."

There are some other ways that friendships change. When our old friends develop new interests, other new friends, or new and different ways of doing things, our friendships are affected and we may not be as close to those friends as we were. You might bring this out by asking the children to respond to such questions as: "Have you ever had a friend not want to play ball with you anymore because he or she liked to do something else now?" or "Have you ever had a friend leave you for another friend?" "How did you feel?" Allow the children time to respond.

Continue the discussion by saying something like this: "We have many feelings, don't we, when our friendships change. Let's look at someone whose life changed because of a move. He had to deal with many friendship changes. His name was Joseph." Ask the children to turn with you in their Bibles to Genesis 37:12-29. Read (or have one of the children read) this story of Joseph being sold and taken to Egypt. After reading the passage, help the children to discuss how Joseph might have felt. You may begin by

Friendship Survey

1. Do you have any acquaintances? If so, what are their names?

_____   _____

_____   _____

_____   _____

2. Do you have friends with whom you play or do things? If you do, what are their names and what are the things you like doing the most when you are together?

Names of Friends with Whom I Play or Do Things   Favorite Activities

_____   _____

_____   _____

_____   _____

_____   _____

3. Do you have any best friends? If you do, what are their names?

_____   _____

NOTE: Most people do not have more than one or two best friends. This is because best friends are hard to find and friendships between best friends require a lot of hard work.

4. List the qualities you like in a friend:

_____   _____

_____   _____

_____   _____

5. Complete the sentences below:

(a.) A friend _____

_____

(b.) A friend never _____

_____

(c.) I like a friend who _____

_____

(d.) My friends _____

_____

(e.) To have friends _____

_____

saying something like this: "How do you suppose Joseph felt when he was taken from his home?" Allow the children to share their feelings. Ask them to write on Friend #1 any responses which do not already appear there.

After the discussion ends, point out to the children that Joseph had to cope with (you may need to define the word "cope," i.e., to handle, work with, live with, etc.) these feelings. In Genesis chapters 39-50 we see that he did cope very well. Because of limited time, instead of reading the chapters, you will need to summarize that Joseph coped in Egypt by:

1. successfully making new friends
2. letting go of the old friends (yet keeping communications open)
3. relying on God's help to see him through the crises

Remind the children that Joseph was so successful in his new home that he actually rose to a position of very great power. Share also with the children that they will be looking at these three ways of coping throughout the rest of the session.

Initiating New Friendships—Dealing with Life-Size Friend #2 (20 minutes)

Begin by labeling Friend #2 with the following phrase: "One way to cope with friendship changes: make new friends." Beforehand, write these five words in bold, colorful letters on 3-by-5-inch (7.7-by-12.8 cm) cards or small pieces of white tag board: *special, important, interested, name,* and *listen.* Pass these cards out to five of the children. Have them hold these until you call for them.

Proceed by explaining to the children that one way to cope with the loss of a friendship is to make new friends. You might say something like this: "But how do we go about making new friends?" Ask the children to take a few minutes to read their survey sheets once again, especially looking at the names of their various kinds of friends (acquaintances, friends with whom they play, and best friends). Ask them to try to remember how they became friends with these people. While the rest of the group is thinking, ask each of the five children, one at a time, to tape his or her card on Friend #2.

Express to the children these thoughts as you point to each of the five cards: "There are several things a person needs to do when making a friend."

1. Pointing to the card with the word "special" on it, say: "The first thing to do when making a friend is to think of the other person as being *special.*"[1] Lead the children in discussion by asking them to recall how they think of their friends. You might say something like this: "Do you think your friends are special?" "How do you show it?"

[1] Adapted from Joy Wilt, *A Kid's Guide to Making Friends* (Waco: Word, Inc., Educational Products Division).

NOTE: For each of the discussion periods (this one and the ones to follow), be sure to record the children's responses to the questions upon Friend #2, for review and summary later on in the session.

2. Pointing to the card with the word "important" on it, say: "The second thing to do when making a friend is to think of the other person as *important.*" Stimulate discussion by asking, "What are some of the things you do to make your friends feel important?"
3. Pointing to the card with the word "interested" on it, say: "The third thing to do when making a friend is to show the other person that you are *interested* in him or her." Ask the children, "How do you show your friends you are interested in them?"
4. Pointing to the card with the word "name" on it, say: "The fourth thing to do when making a friend is to remember that a person's name is very important. Do you call your friends by their names as often as you can?" Perhaps the children could share their friends' names with you and the total group.
5. Pointing to the card with the word "listen" on it, say: "The fifth thing to do when making a friend is to be a good *listener.*" Again, you may begin the discussion by asking, "Do you listen carefully to your friends and encourage them to talk about themselves?"

After finishing the fifth card, ask the children if they would like to add any other ways to make a friend. Allow time for the children to respond and be sure to thank them for their contributions. End this time by reviewing and summarizing all that is listed on Friend #2. Be careful to point out that if the children are doing these things with their friends already, it probably won't be hard for them to make new friends when the need should arise. Stress once again that making new friends is one way of coping (dealing) with their feelings when an old friendship changes.

Letting Go—Friendship Notes (15 minutes)

Convey to the children that, though making new friends helps when we lose old friends, we still need to cope with missing those friends. Sometimes one just can't replace a friend. (I'm not sure we should even try.) Sometimes we need to let go of friendships because people live too far away, but we can still keep in touch. Ask the children something like this: "How many of you have friends who live far away?" "How do you keep in touch with them?" (You may get such responses as: by phone, visits, letters, notes, etc.)

Suggest (if it hasn't come up already) that one way to cope with missing our friends is to write them notes. Allow the children to pick out one of the friends who has moved away, and write a note to him or her. While passing out paper and pencils, explain to the children that this can be done in many different ways and that they can decide how they wish to do this project. Make these suggestions: It could be a note to say goodbye, a note telling their friend how much they like him or her, a note to say thank you for something, a note listing all the things they like about their friend, a note asking about their new home, a note telling about old times, a note to cheer up their friend or just a note to say "Hi."[2] When the children have finished writing, invite those who would wish to do so, to share their compositions. Share as many of them as time will permit.

Closing Activity

Sharing a Litany—Asking for God's Help (5 minutes)

After making sure the children are comfortable, begin by emphasizing that a third way of coping with friendship changes is to live the best we can right where we are, to "bloom where we are planted," so to speak. Sometimes we need help in order to be strong when we lose a friend, or to face moving to a different house, school, city, church. God can give us that strength, that help.

[2] Adapted from Wayne Rice, ed., *Ideas No. 28*, copyright 1978 by Youth Specialties, 1224 Greenfield Drive, El Cajon, CA 92021.

In closing, invite the children to share the following litany with you from Isaiah 41:10 (TEV). You may want to have the litany printed for each of the children ahead of time. You or one of the children will read the "Leader" verses and the rest of the group will read the response: "Thank you, God, for being our helper."

Litany
Leader: Do not be afraid—I am with you!
Response: Thank you, God, for being our helper.
Leader: I am your God—let nothing terrify you!
Response: Thank you, God, for being our helper.
Leader: I will make you strong and help you;
Response: Thank you, God, for being our helper.
Leader: I will protect you and save you.
Response: Thank you, God, for being our helper.

Bible Used in This Session: Genesis 37:12-29, Isaiah 41:10, TEV

Session 2

I Want to Be Like My Friends

Purpose

- To help children become aware of who they are and to encourage the uniqueness of each person in an age of peer pressure and conformity.
- To help children discover ways of understanding and dealing with parental rules and restrictions and to begin to recognize their own responsibilites, choices, and decisions better.

Background for Leader(s)

When a child says to you, "I want to be like my friends," what do you suppose he or she is really saying? I think we need to try to assess what actually is going on inside the child's mind. What anxieties, frustrations, and questions should we be addressing? In this session we will be briefly touching on the following areas:

1. Self-esteem
2. Individuality and uniqueness
3. Peer pressure
4. Parents—what they will and won't allow
5. What the Bible says is the child's responsibility

Self-Esteem

How children feel about themselves dictates the standards they set for their own behavior. As they grow, their inner feelings or "consciences" usually tell them what is right for them. Virtue, in this world, is not always rewarded in kind. Children must be helped to realize that the reward they can expect from moral behavior will come principally from within themselves and from the respect and love of those whom they, in turn, respect and love. To protect children from drug abuse, for example, we must nurture within them high self-esteem. High self-esteem can help a child say: "I am proud to be me . . . and because I am proud, I will take care of myself, especially my body. I won't put anything into it that will hurt me."

High self-esteem is based on children's believing that they are lovable and worthwhile. Children must know that they matter, *just because they exist.* They need to feel competent to handle themselves and their environment and must feel they have something to offer others. High self-esteem is not conceit. It is feeling a quiet comfort about being *who* they are.

Individuality and Uniqueness

We need to determine whether children place a high priority and value on individuality and uniqueness in their view of themselves. If they do, we need to reinforce that way of thinking. If not, we need to help the children see the importance of being themselves and of thinking their own thoughts and celebrating their own unique ways of being in the world.

Peer Pressure

In an attempt to establish identities of their own, children will sometimes look indiscriminately to their friends for cues as to what they "should" do and how they "should" behave. This is, of course, what we call "peer pressure" to conform. It is our job, once again, to reinforce and help children to value their own God-given uniqueness. We need to help them to appreciate their individuality and to clarify the difference between healthy and unhealthy responses to everyday realities and situations. We need to help them choose, for example, not to go along with the crowd just to be popular or well liked, but to choose from their own set of values and according to the rules and regulations that their parents have asked them to obey.

Parents—What They Will and Won't Allow

Values of the child's parents or of other significant adults in the child's life are more important than we often realize. Children will make these values their own if adults have truly done so themselves. Moralizing and preaching won't do much good unless children see that adults live by what they are saying.

It is important, at this age, to set limits that will protect children from problems that they are not yet able to handle on their own. We need not run down or oppose the children's judgments. We can just make it clear that we feel there are certain situations they cannot handle yet all by themselves. Most children appreciate the firmness and being told that they are valued by the limits we set for them.

What the Bible Says Is the Child's Responsibility

Ephesians 6:1-3 helps us to understand that it is important for children to see that the biblical imperative for them is to obey their parents: "Children, it is your Christian duty to obey your parents, for this is the right thing to do.

'Respect your father and mother' is the first commandment that has a promise added: 'so that all may go well with you, and you may live a long time in the land' '' (TEV).

Sometimes it is hard for children to obey—in fact hard for people of any age. If parents are seeking, in love, what is good for their children and are obeying God's imperative for them (bringing them up with loving discipline), truly the rewards will be satisfying.

Beginning Activity

Finding Out About "Me" (15 minutes)

After welcoming each child, ask the boys and girls to sit at tables where you have already placed felt-tip pens (in a variety of colors) and white paper for each child. Explain to the children that you would like them to draw pictures of themselves and how they feel about themselves today (i.e., happy, sad, energetic, tired, etc.). Allow time for the

children to draw, explaining too that "today we will be talking about how we feel about ourselves, our self-esteem. Do we feel confident (sure), happy, secure, or not so confident, not so happy, not so secure?"

Allow the children about five minutes for drawing. Then share and talk about the pictures. Be sure to comment on such things as happy faces, sunshine, bright colors, or different activities that the children have pictured. Be sure to emphasize that it is very important to have, or to learn to have, a good image of ourselves. It is important to learn to be confident in what we believe, because sometime we may have to stand all alone and do what we think is right even if no one else agrees. Or, we may need to say "no" when someone asks us to do something we feel is wrong.

Developing Activities

Peer Pressure Inventory (15 minutes)

Allow the children to sit in a circle in front of a newsprint or blackboard displaying this heading: "Friends Pressure Us To. . . ." Begin by asking the children whether they have ever been asked to do anything they felt it would be wrong to do. On newsprint or blackboard compile a list from their comments. You may get such varied suggestions

as: pick flowers in someone else's garden, go back into the school building when we're not allowed, steal candy from the corner store, or try drugs. Be sure to allow time to ask them such questions as: "How did you feel when your friend asked you to do that?" or "How did you handle the situation?" or "How would you like to have handled it?" Allow the children time to respond. Be careful not to be judgmental or critical and be sure to reinforce the children for the times they said "no" to their friends and stood up for what they felt was right. Emphasize again that it is important to feel good about ourselves. It is OK to be unique, special, even different, to have a sureness (confidence) about ourselves and what we believe. Then we can better stand alone, apart from the crowd, and think our own thoughts and live our own values. Our friends will not influence us so much in what we say and what we do if we are confident in ourselves. (It also helps when we have lots of support, love, and sound training from our parents.)

How Much of an Individual Are You?—The Great Button Controversy[1] (10 minutes)

As an object lesson on conformity, put ten buttons (or pennies) in a box and pass them around the group. Have each child count the buttons and remember how many there were in the box. They are not to tell anyone what their count is just yet. By prior arrangement, the next-to-the-last person removes one button from the box secretly (or you can do it) so that the last person's count is off by one. When the children have finished, ask each child how many buttons he or she counted. It is hoped that everyone will agree except for the last person. Congratulate the person, if he or she *does* stand alone, pointing out that he or she has withstood peer pressure and probably has a pretty high degree of self-esteem. In all probability, though, the different person will change the count to conform to the others, even though he or she is sure of being right. If this be the case, you might follow up with a further discussion on group pressure and the temptation to deny our personal convictions in order to be accepted by our peers.

[1] Adapted from Wayne Rice, ed., *Ideas #9-12*, page 76. Used by permission from *Ideas*, copyright 1978 by Youth Specialties, 1224 Greenfield Dr., El Cajon, CA 92021.

Parental Inventory I (15 minutes)

Using a blackboard and chalk, or newsprint and felt-tip pen, display this heading: "What Our Parents Allow Us to Do." (Note: The purpose of this inventory is to show that parents don't just say "no" to everything all the time, but do allow their children to do things and also that parents respect their children and appreciate their abilities by giving them responsibilites in the form of privileges, tasks, and jobs.) Begin by asking the children to share what their parents (or guardians) allow them to do. The children will be eager to share with you and the total group, in a popcorn style, by raising their hands and being called on. They may share such things as: mowing the lawn, drying dishes, vacuuming, checking on the baby, going to the store, taking care of the dog, etc. Be sure to praise them for their jobs well done. Point out that they should be proud that their parents trust and respect them so much that they allow them such positions of responsibility. List all their responses carefully on the newsprint or blackboard under the heading. You may want to ask questions about how they go about doing their jobs.

Parental Inventory II (15 minutes)

Begin this section by saying something like this: "Now I'm going to ask you to switch gears for a moment. What are some of the things your parents *don't* allow you to do?" Display these headings on newsprint or on a blackboard.

RESTRIC-TIONS (What my parents don't allow me to do)	REASONS	FAIR OR UNFAIR	MY RESPON-SIBILITY
Example:			
1. To go to my friend's house without permission.	Parents will worry	F, but also U, at times	To obey my parents but talk with them about my feelings

Again, have the children share in a popcorn style by raising their hands to be called on. (You will be surprised at their enthusiasm over this.) List the children's responses in Column 1 ("Restrictions"). You may receive such replies as: to go to my friend's house without permission, to go out in the cold or rain without proper clothes, to go out into Dad's workshop when he is not there, etc. As each child gives you a restriction, ask the child also: "Why do you suppose your mom or dad set up that rule?" Help the child (or solicit the help of the total group) to come up with a "reason." Write (or have the child write) the reason in Column 2 under the heading, "Reasons." After all the children who wish to share have done so, point to Column 3 and say something like this: "Let's see how some of you feel about these rules. Are they fair or unfair?" For each rule record the responses of the children, using a "U" (unfair) or an "F" (fair) or appropriate comments. Discuss

the responses, as needed, perhaps using a question such as: "Why do you feel that rule is unfair?"

Sharing from God's Word (15 minutes)

Before the children can look at their responsibilities in relation to their parents' rules and restrictions, they need to see what God's Word says about obeying their parents. Allow the children time to look up Ephesians 6:1-3 in their own Bibles or ones you have provided for them. (Note: Some of the children may need help in finding the passage.) It is also helpful to have the passage written in large, colorful letters, right in front of the children, perhaps displayed on posterboard.

After reading the verses, discuss what these verses might mean (i.e., being an obedient child—what does that mean for them?). Ask the children to look at Column 4 ("My Responsibility"). Share with the children that it is often easier to obey those restrictions that seem fair and reasonable to them. But ask them how they feel about obeying the restrictions they feel are unfair or unreasonable. Do they find it harder to obey their parents when their friends want them to do something else? (It might be helpful to find a problem item on the inventory and use it as an example.) Help the children see that they *are* to obey their parents. At the same time children need to feel that they may communicate their feelings to their parents. In fact, children should be encouraged to do so.

Closing Prayer (5 minutes)

Allow the children time to stretch for a bit and then ask them to gather in a circle to pray together a prayer of thanksgiving. Guide them in thanking God for their parents (or those who care for them), for making each of them unique and special and asking God to help them to be obedient children.

Bible Used in This Session: Ephesians 6:1-3

Session 3

Being a Friend in a Difficult Time

Purpose
- To help children realize that in and through difficult times God loves and cares for them.
- To help children become aware of how to help a friend who is going through a difficult time.

Background for Leader(s)

Why do "bad" things happen to "good" people? Have you ever asked yourself that question? Why must people suffer? Why must those we love die? Why do people argue, fight, and even kill each other? Why do married couples separate and divorce? Why? Why? Why? We, as adults, have trouble with these difficult dilemmas. Can you imagine what a time children must have? How can we live in such a broken world? We cannot attempt to answer these questions within this session, but it is important to raise them. When difficult times come for a child in a family, like the death of a parent or a separation or a divorce, there are myriads of feelings, thoughts, and emotions that the child will experience. Feelings such as loneliness, frustration, sadness, anger, abandonment, rejection, hopelessness, and despair are just a few. Questions can arise, too, about where God is in all of this. Does God care? Does God still love me?

The focus of this session will be on a caring and loving God. We will be helping the children realize that in difficulties God *does know* what is happening and *does care* about and *love* us. God promises to be with us in and through the difficult times, to strengthen, guide, and support us. We can claim the promises contained in the following verses. Each verse is paraphrased.

- Jeremiah 29:11, 13, . . . The plans God has made for us include prosperity and hope.
- Romans 8:28, 38-39, Nothing can separate us from the love of God.
- Isaiah 41:10, Don't be afraid. God makes us strong and will help us.
- Matthew 28:20, I will be with you always, even to the end of the age.
- Joshua 1:9, Be determined and confident—don't be afraid or discouraged, because God is with us wherever we go.
- Psalm 116:15, God's loved ones are very precious to God.

- Psalm 34:18, The Lord is near to those who are discouraged; God saves those who have lost all hope.
- Philippians 4:13, I have the strength to face all conditions by the power Christ gives me.

It is important for children and adults alike to realize that, although God allows our world to be broken by sin and its consequences, God is still there to care for us and help us through the difficult times. If the only thing the children learn in this session is that God knows and God cares for them, we have done our job.

We need to go one step further, however. We must help children to see how they can help a friend in a difficult time. Let me share with you four steps that may be helpful as you guide the children in this area.

When a Friend Is Going Through a Difficult Time

(Note: These are probably not the words you would use with the children. These are guidelines in a general form for adults as well.)

Step 1: Be available.
- —This guideline is the most important; if you do nothing else at first, do this one.
- —Listen to your friend.
- —Get a clear picture of what is happening to your friend. Be sure to get in touch with his or her feelings.

Step 2: Assure your friend that God knows and cares.
- —Know what God's Word says and be ready and able sensitively to share God's promises of love and provision with your friend, should the need arise. (Note: Be careful to explain to the children that they should not just "spout off" the verses without thinking or because they think it is the "thing to do." It's important to wait until their friend is ready to listen and hear. Sometimes it might be best to wait until their friend asks for such assurance.)

Step 3: Pray.
- —Pray *with* your friend. But pray only if it is appropriate and helpful for your friend (i.e., according to your friend's needs, not because you feel it is the "right thing to do").

—Pray for your friend. One can always pray at home, claiming the promise, strength, support, and guidance of God for a friend. (You might remind the children that this type of prayer, intercessory prayer, is very powerful in its effect.)

Step 4: Do something for your friend!

—If you are really listening, your friend will tell you what he or she needs.

—If you can, do what needs to be done. (Remind the children that they can't do everything, but there is usually something they can do, even though it is small: i.e., go for a walk with the friend, help with a chore or a difficult task, clean the friend's room, take care of the friend's favorite dog or cat, etc.)

Being a friend in a difficult time may often involve more listening than talking, more just "being there" than doing. But, first and foremost, it involves being sensitive to what your friend needs and to what God is asking you to do. The greatest gift of all is that, as Christians, we can bring with us the very power and presence of Christ to our friends. All we need to do is to be there and be open and listen to God and to our friend's needs. We must be willing to be used by a mighty and loving God. We cannot expect that children will learn how to do this all at once, and certainly not in this session; this takes a lifetime of learning. Children will be introduced to the idea of being present. Children have a special way of being ministers of Christ and bringing his presence wherever they go just by being who they are.

Beginning Activity

Reminders of God's Love (15 minutes)

After welcoming the children, allow them to sit on the floor in a circle in front of you. Sit down with them and share something like this (with your Bible in hand): "Today, let's think about the special times when we are aware of God or are reminded of God's love. Let me share this verse from God's Word." Read Jeremiah 29:13 from your Bible: "You will seek me, and you will find me because you will seek me with all your heart" (TEV). Explain that God has promised that, if we look, we will find God in our everyday world. You might say something like: "I would like you to think of your day, so far. Look for the times, places, experiences where you could see or feel God's presence. Perhaps in the sun shining in your bedroom window this morning or perhaps in a hug from Mom or Dad. Maybe you felt God's presence while you were praying this morning or last night or sometime during the day." Give each child a 3-by-5-inch (7.7-by-12.8 cm) card and ask each to write down the times or places they were reminded of God's love and presence. Allow time to think and to write. As they are doing this, put the verse (Jeremiah 29:13) on a newsprint sheet in front of the group. This could be printed ahead of time and put up now.

As the children finish, allow them to talk about their cards and then tape them up on newsprint under the Scripture verse. Summarize by sharing other concrete ways through which we know that God is present in our lives.

Developing Activities

Feelings Collage (15 minutes)

After finishing the discussion of "Reminders of God's Love," ask one or two of the children to place a collection of magazine pictures which you have cut out ahead of time, on the floor in front of your group. These pictures should depict people in various situations of difficulty: crying, alone, unhappy, sad, arguing, fighting, angry, etc. Try to find some that might be depicting a funeral or a single-parent family. Have other children pass out a preselected collection of crisis and feeling words. These will be words you have cut from magazines or newspapers or that you have printed up yourself on white strips of paper. Such words as "divorce," "death," "funeral," "alone," "sad," "frustrated," "mad," "confused," "lonely," "wondering," and "why" could be used. Also, have on hand blank strips of paper and felt-tip markers for the children to write their own words to add to the collection.

As the children are passing out the materials, suggest something like this: "We've just finished sharing our experiences of how we know God is present in our lives. We must be aware of this as we talk about *how to be a friend in times that are difficult.* Knowing that God is present in our lives is valuable, not only in the good times but also in the difficult times, and especially when we are trying to help our friends go through times that are rough." Continue by saying something like this: "Let's look at some of the pictures we have here in front of us. Maybe they can help us get in touch with some of the difficult things that can happen to our friends and how they might be feeling. Let's make a collage." Provide a posterboard or paper and glue. Allow the children to paste on it pictures they have selected from the collection in front of them. Ask them to describe what might be going on in the picture (i.e., "They're fighting," "She's crying," "She is looking sad," etc.) You might elicit even more responses if you not only ask "What are they doing in the picture?" but also "How do you suppose he or she is feeling in this picture?" or "What do you think might have just happened here?" Remember there is no "right" answer; just encourage the children to respond. Allow the children to paste words by the pictures to describe what they think is going on and what the people in the pictures are feeling. These may be words they have found in the collection or ones they have written on the blank strips of paper.

After they have finished, summarize what the children have discovered to be some of the difficulties that could happen to our friends. Continue by saying something like this: "Sometimes the difficult things that happen to our friends could seem like too much to bear. Our purpose today, though, is not to dwell so much on the things that are difficult, but to focus on God's presence, love, and help in our times of trouble and sorrow. Let's take some time now to look to God's Word for what God has promised for us as God's children.

Sharing from God's Word (15 minutes)

Print the following verses on strips of colored construction paper. You may have these prepared ahead of time or ask the children to prepare them during the session.

God's Promises

1. Nothing can separate us from God's love (Romans 8:38-39).
2. God is with us and makes us strong (Isaiah 41:10, Philippians 4:13, Matthew 28:20).
3. We are precious to God (Psalm 116:15).
4. God's plans for us are good (Jeremiah 29:11).

Read the Bible verses or have the children read them. As you do, discuss with the children how these promises and truths can be very helpful and comforting for them and for their friends as they go through difficult times. Allow the children to tape the verses on the "Feelings Collage." When they have finished putting the verses on the collage, suggest that the pictures of difficulties look a bit different now. You might say something like this: "The troubles and problems are still here (point to a picture or two), the feelings are still here (point to a few feeling words), but God is here, too (point to a few promises), helping us in and through our difficult times. This is probably one of the most important things we can share with our friends—the truth that, when they are going through times of trouble, God is there and God cares."

Finger Puppets (40 minutes)

Allow the children a few minutes to stretch. Then divide them into two groups. Share something like this: "Now we're going to use what we've just learned. We're going to act out a play using finger puppets. We're going to make up two plays about friends of ours who are going through hard and difficult times. For Group 1 the friend has just had one of his parents die. For Group 2 the friend's parents have just gotten a divorce. Your friends have asked you to come over to help."

Provide the children with four steps to follow when preparing their plays. Place the steps on newsprint and read them to the children. Ask them to show as many of the steps as they can in their plays.

Four Steps to Follow When Being a Friend in a Difficult Time[1]

1. Go to your friend and listen. Find out how he or she is feeling and what he or she needs.
2. Share with the friend that God cares and will help.

[1]NOTE: Please refer to "Background for Leader(s)" in this session, for how to handle these four steps.

3. Pray *with* and *for* your friend.
4. Do something with and for your friend.

Allow time to explain the four steps and help the children discover how they can depict them in their plays. Provide also four old gloves (two for each group), felt-tip markers, yarn, glue, cardboard, construction paper, felt, etc., for making the puppets. Allow the children time to construct the puppets. Cut off the tips of the fingers on the gloves.

Draw eyes and noses and mouths on the tips; the children may want to use the yarn or felt for hair.[2] They will need enough puppets to portray themselves, their friends, and their friends' families. The children may want to make a stage from a cardboard square. To do this they will need to cut out the middle of the square and attach curtains on each side of the opening. They will only need to make one stage, since both groups can share it.

Allow each group time to prepare. You need to be available for advice and/or suggestions. After the groups have finished, allow time for each to share its play. Use this experience for more discussion and sharing. Be sure to thank all of the children for their participation and work.

Closing Prayer (5 minutes)

Gather the children together in a circle. Sit on the floor, and allow them time to settle down after the play presentations. Lead them in a prayer of thanksgiving for God's love, presence, and help, especially in times of need.

Bible Used in This Session: Jeremiah 29:11, 13; Romans 8:28, 38-39; Isaiah 41:10; Joshua 1:9; Psalm 116:15; 34:18; Philippians 4:13; Matthew 28:20

[2]The illustration and instructions for making finger puppets are adapted from Freeda Gates, *Glove, Mitten, and Sock Puppets* (New York: Walker & Company, Inc.).

Session 4

Our Family Was Already Big Enough

Purpose

- To help children get in touch with their feelings when someone new comes into their family.
- To help children discover that they have a very special and unique position of value as a child of God.

Background for Leader(s)

What happens to children when a new baby arrives to live in their home? Some children find the advent of a baby very exciting. They—especially young girls—see the new arrival as cute, cuddly, or fun to play with. For others, however, the new baby is a threat, an intrusion. The baby's arrival is seen as a crisis and an unsettling time, in which the child's very self is questioned. Thoughts sometimes arise in a child's mind like: "Will Mom and Dad still love me?" "Will I have to share my room, my toys?" "Will I like the new baby?" "Wasn't I a good enough child?" "Did we need another one?"

Reactions to a new baby in the family may be many and varied. The other children may whine, cry, be angry or demanding, try to injure the young baby, or suddenly exhibit obnoxious behavior. They may become depressed, moody, jealous, or distressed in the belief that all of their parents' attention is going to the intruder. They may start violating house rules or may long to go back to a time when less was asked of them and they felt more secure. They may pause in their growth or, if they were about to take a new step, they may put if off until they are more sure of things. At this time, such children need to be loved just *where they are* and for *who they are* and most of all, they do not need any added pressures.

Adults can help in such a crisis by admiring children for their own specialness and uniqueness, for how they have grown, what they already can do, and what good company they are. We can also give the children the story of their own babyhood (whenever possible). To each child the story of his or her own beginning tells who he or she is, where he or she comes from, and to whom he or she belongs. Psalm 139:1-16 will also help children to see that, no matter how large the family might be, they are still seen and known and very special in God's eyes. God always cares and has time for us.

We as adults can also provide an arena whereby children can be accepted unconditionally and helped to learn to share

their relationships with family members. We can help children learn the joys of being able to know and experience another person. We can help them to know that by God's grace and love they can be equipped to face and conquer some of their own worst fears.

This session deals mostly with what happens when a new baby arrives in the home, but there are other kinds of newcomers who enter the family circle. Some children may be dealing with similar emotions, feelings, and reactions in these new relationships. They may be facing a situation such as Grandpa or Grandma coming to live with them or stepchildren from a previous marriage moving in.

In teaching this session, keep in mind that, when children accept and like themselves, it is much easier for them to like others. When they are encouraged to grow in their own unique way, they can allow others to grow in *their* ways. When children are sure of their beginnings, they can let another have a beginning, too. When they are sure there is room for them in their family and that they belong, they are more ready to make room for a new person in the family.

Beginning Activity

Time to Draw (20 minutes)

After welcoming the children, have them sit comfortably at a table where you have already placed a piece of white typing paper or drawing paper and a variety of crayons or felt-tip pens for each child. Explain to them that we will be talking about our families today and how families sometimes change. Ask them to tell how many they each have in their families. You might also say something like this: "Have any of you ever had a new brother or sister come to your house? How did you feel?" After a few of them have shared, explain what they are about to do with the paper and pens in front of them. You may wish to say something like this: "I would like you to draw a picture of your family. Include all the persons in your family, just as you see them. Be sure to draw yourself, too." Allow the children time to draw (about 10 minutes). Circulate among the children and offer help and praise as they work.

After they have finished, allow them to share their pictures with the group, if they feel comfortable doing so. Encourage those who share to tell who the people are and where they fit into their family. You might ask them how they feel about being in their family. Most children this age will say

"fine" or "I feel happy," when perhaps they are not. You might also look for such things as rainbows or suns shining or bright colors which often denote happy experiences. A child using all black, for example, may not be feeling too happy in his or her family. If a child leaves out certain family members, that might indicate some uncomfortable feelings or experiences with the person or persons who are left out of the drawing. You might watch, too, for size relationships. It is common for a child to draw Mom and Dad larger than himself or herself and a baby sister or brother smaller. On the other hand, a child may draw everyone the same size, possibly signifying that he or she feels totally equal and accepted in the family. If a child draws everyone larger than herself or himself, this may indicate how small the child really feels. You might simply end this time by thanking each child for his or her hard work and good drawings.

Developing Activities

Let's Pretend—Role Plays (40 minutes)

In advance equip a cardboard box, a clothes trunk, or a clothes tree with these items, or ones that are similar, for two role plays:

Role Play 1: A New Baby
—a baby doll
—a man's hat
—a woman's hat
—a child's sweater

Role Play 2: Grandpa's Moving In
—a child's jacket or shirt
—a child's game
—a man's vest or shirt
—a cane

Put the trunk or box or tree in a spacious corner of your room with a large oval or square rug spread out before it (or mark off an area with masking tape) to be used as a "stage" for the role plays.

Begin by asking the children to come with you to a place where "we can pretend." Say something like this as you lead them to the corner you have already prepared: "This is a very special place where we can put on clothes and pretend we are different people in a different family." Have the children sit on the stage area. Then proceed to take out the props for Role Play 1. You might say something like this: "Let's see what we have in our trunk—a baby doll, a man's hat, a woman's hat, and a child's sweater." (Hold up each of the items as you mention them.) "Who would like to help with our first role play?" After selecting the appropriate number of volunteers, share the description and allow the children time for comments and/or questions. Then ask those who have volunteered to use the props to conduct a five-minute role play for the group. Introduce and set up Role Play 2 in the same way as the first. After both role plays have been introduced and set up, allow the children time to think of what they are going to do. Perhaps you and the total group can help with ideas. When the volunteers are ready, have them present the role plays they have prepared. Be ready and available to help and advise where needed.

Observe the reactions, responses, and comments of the children as they enact the role plays. Do not hesitate to stop them and have a discussion when it seems appropriate. Allow time for a discussion after each role play is finished. Help the children get in touch with how it feels when a new person comes into a family. You might ask something like: "How do you suppose _____felt or _____felt when someone new came into the family?" Allow time for the children to share.

Description of Role Play 1: A New Baby

In this role play, _____is anxiously awaiting the arrival of Mom and Dad from the hospital with their new baby. This is the first time _____will have seen the baby. ____ is not sure how _____feels. When Mom and Dad come through the door, _____rushes to meet them. Show how you think _____would act and feel when Mom asks "What do you think of your new sister?" and Dad says, "Would you like to hold her?" and both parents want to know if there is anything _____"would like to talk about."

Description of Role Play 2: Grandpa's Moving In

In this role play, Grandpa has just moved into _____ family's home. _____is an only child and used to having things _____own way. Grandpa comes into _____ room where _____is playing with a favorite game. Show how you think _____would act and feel when Grandpa moves into _____room and needs to share things.

Leader's Note: We have left the names blank so that either a boy or girl could feel free to volunteer for the role play in either situation. You need to fill in the blanks appropriately when you know who will be doing the role play.

Feelings—What to Do with Them (15 minutes)

As you continue to talk over the role plays, help the children to see that many different feelings happen to us when a new person moves into a family. List the ones you've already shared and the ones you will be discovering on a newsprint labeled "Feelings." One might feel angry or jealous or not too secure when the new baby arrives. One may be frustrated or mad at having to share with a grandparent. On the other hand, one may be very happy to share and excited to have someone new to talk to and be with. Some of these feelings are comfortable ones and others are uncomfortable.

Continue by saying something like this: "Here are some important things to remember when looking at feelings." Have the following written on newsprint for the children to see:

Important Things to Remember About Feelings[1]

We need to:
1. Accept our feelings rather than try not to have them.
2. Understand that God created us as individual persons, and therefore we have all kinds of feelings. Therefore God will help us with all of our feelings.
3. Realize it is what we do about our feelings that is important.
4. Understand that uncomfortable feelings can:
   a. make us do the things that need to be done;
   b. make us grow and change for the better;
   c. help us appreciate comfortable feelings.

While you are talking about items on the newsprint and afterward, allow the children time for questions, comments, and discussion. It is often difficult for children to know and identify their own feelings. Therefore, it is important that we help them to do so. Feelings tell them a great deal about the kinds of persons they are and need to be.

Closing Activity

Sharing from God's Word—A Litany of Thanksgiving (15 minutes)

Begin by saying something like this: "Let's see what God's Word tells us about how very special and important we are to God. It doesn't matter how many people there are in our families or what we might be feeling about that right now; we are special and important to God." Have the children turn to Psalm 139:1-4, 13, 17-18, and follow along as you or one of the children read. After you have finished

[1] Adapted from Joy Wilt, *Handling Your Ups and Downs* (Waco, Tex.: Word, Inc., Educational Products Division).

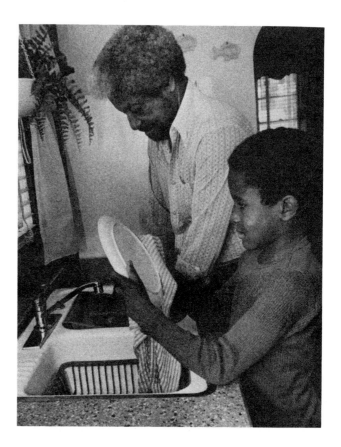

reading, allow time for comments and discussion. Then invite the children to share with you a closing Litany of Thanksgiving (freely adapted from Psalm 139). They will read the response, "Thank you, Lord," after you read the leader portions. (You might want to duplicate copies for each child.)

Litany of Thanksgiving

Leader: O Lord, you know everything about me. You know when I sit or stand. You know my every thought.
Response: Thank you, Lord!
Leader: Every moment, you know where I am. You are constantly thinking about me.
Response: Thank you, Lord!
Leader: You know what I am going to say before I even say it.
Response: Thank you, Lord!
Leader: You place your hand of blessing on my head.
Response: Thank you, Lord!
Leader: You made all the delicate, inner parts of my body. Thank you for making me. . . .
Response: Thank you, Lord!

Bible Used in This Session: Psalm 139:1-4, 13, 17-18

We're All Hurt When Someone's Sick

Purpose
- To identify the realities involved when there is long-term sickness in the family and to help children express their feelings.
- To help children become aware of the coping skills for dealing with illness in the family.

Background for Leader(s)

What are the effects of long-term sickness in the family? Certainly the most pronounced is a preoccupation with illness and with the sick person. Time, energy, and money are spent to care for and entertain and to try to cure the ill parent or child. If a sibling is terminally ill, for example, the other children in the family may suffer from lack of attention, less quality time with their parents, abnormal schedules, uptight parents, out-of-control situations and living environments, less time for fun, more responsibilities, less money to spend, having to be quiet, having people feeling sorry for them, many hospital visits, etc. Also, they might have to deal with feelings such as anger, frustration, jealousy, fear of death of the sick person, fear of abandonment, envy, guilt (for evil thoughts, or just for being happy), depression, sadness, lack of control over the situation, insecurity, instability, and unsureness that they are loved—just to name a few.

Most of these feelings are uncomfortable. In the early years, children learn more about how to handle their uncomfortable feelings from watching how adults deal with theirs than by all the preaching in the world. Children must learn from us to confront their problems seriously and not look for easy but unsatisfactory remedies.

We all hurt when someone is sick. Many of the children in your group may not have experienced, or may never experience, such a crisis. The purpose of this session is not to frighten the children but to aid them in getting in touch with the realities of illness. They need to realize that illness does go on in families and that perhaps, if their family does not experience it, they will see it in a friend's or relative's family.

In all fairness, the fact must be addressed that, though there are many uncomfortable feelings to deal with when someone in our family is sick, there are also many corresponding comfortable feelings. For example, feelings of happiness in special moments spent together as a family

. . . the happy experiences of being loved, appreciated, needed, and useful . . . learning to share and feeling that things don't have to be ''perfect'' in order to have fun . . . treasuring the small things, a wink, a smile, a hug, a walk, a talk that says ''I love you!'' . . . a closeness to God, relying on God for support and comfort and strength. These things can be found and experienced, if we choose to look for them. We learn that within the crisis itself there is joy, laughter, and, yes, even good times!

Beginning Activity

Story Box (30 minutes)

After welcoming the children, direct them to a central location where they can sit in a circle (on the floor or in chairs, comfortably). Then you need to sit where they can see you. Have the story box with you.

You will need to have prepared beforehand a story box that contains:

—six clothespin figures (faces drawn with felt-tip pens, clothes made out of felt or other cloth) including one girl (10 years old), one father, one mother, one small boy (5 years old), one boy (10 years old), one doctor
—two beds (made out of wood or cardboard—or use real doll furniture) with cloth blankets and pillows
—two windows (made out of cardboard or construction paper), one bedroom window with the sun shining through, one dining room window (perhaps a picture window)
—one table (made out of wood blocks or cardboard—or doll furniture) with five chairs
—one stairway, made out of blocks or cardboard (optional)

Begin by sharing with the children that we will be talking about what happens when someone in the family is very sick for a long time. You might ask whether any of the children has ever had a family member who was (or is) very sick. If some of them respond, ask them to tell about their experiences if they feel comfortable doing so. (You may find that children will share about someone who has a cold or the flu, etc. Help them to distinguish this from what we are talking about today—long-term illness.)

Then share this story. Either read it or tell it in your own words, using the figures and props from the story box.

This is Emily (clothespin figure in bed). She is ten years old and right now she is still asleep. But she will be waking soon from her sleep, in a happy mood. The sun is shining through her bedroom window (use the cardboard window with the sun shining through) and she just knows that she is going to have a good day. Today is the day her friend Timothy is coming over, and Dad has promised they will go to the park and then get some ice cream. Emily goes downstairs (cardboard stairs) and into the dining room. She walks right up to Paul as he lies in his hospital bed by the picture window (a clothespin figure in bed by a cardboard window). She gives him a kiss and says, "Good morning." Paul responds with a grin.

"He always has such a beautiful smile!" she thinks as she slips into her chair for breakfast. (Use the premade table and chairs.)

Emily is deep in thought as Mom is out in the kitchen making breakfast. Mom has been up early with Paul because he needs lots of care. Dad is still upstairs getting ready, so Emily uses the time just to sit quietly.

Things have changed a lot in their family since Paul has been sick. He has something wrong with his blood and will be sick for a very long time. Sometimes he looks very weak, and Emily knows that Paul is often in a lot of pain, even though he smiles a lot. Sometimes his condition makes Emily feel very sad. She tries to help and will often tell Paul stories and read him books. Paul is only five years old and can't read yet. Oh, how he loves to have Emily read to him! Emily loves it when Paul giggles at a funny picture or asks her to read the story again. Sometimes they have special moments together like this morning when she kissed him and he smiled back at her, saying in his own way, "I love you, Emily!" Or the special times Emily shares her poetry with Paul. She often goes to her room where she can be alone and write poetry for a while. This helps her to sort out her feelings. She shares them only with her brother Paul. He is so good to listen and he seems to understand.

Emily's thoughts are interrupted as Mom comes into the room. (Use the clothespin figure.) Emily thinks that Mom looks tired as she bends down to give her a big hug and kiss. She asks what Emily wants for breakfast. "I've made pancakes. Would you like some?" she asks.

"Oh, yes. That's my favorite, Mom. You bet!" Emily replies.

Emily knows that Mom can't spend as much time with her as she did before Paul became sick. Times like right now make up for that—a favorite breakfast together. Mom winks at Paul as she goes to get Emily's breakfast.

It is nice having Paul here in the dining room, although at first it seemed awkward to Emily. Now it's quite natural and even fun. Dad comes in and gives first Paul and then Emily a "good morning" kiss. Mom sits down and they all sing "God Is So Good!" for their morning prayer. Paul sings, too, as they reach over to hold his hands.

"Boy," Emily thinks, "We really are a special family!" She feels very proud and happy.

After breakfast, Dad asks Emily if she knows what day it is.

"Sure do," she replies. "Park Day!"

"Dad always seems to know what I need before I even ask," Emily thinks.

"You're right," says Dad. "In fact, here's Timmy now."

Timmy comes bouncing in the door (use clothespin figure).

He happily says, "Hi!" to Paul and sits down at the table giving Emily, Mom, and Dad a nod of greeting and then quickly shifts his attention to the leftover pancakes.

"Had any breakfast yet, Tim?" Dad asks.

"Yes, sir, but I could squeeze in one pancake, I reckon," Tim responds.

So, while Tim fills his empty parts, Emily goes over to tell Paul where she is going and promises to bring him a "wee surprise present" when she returns. Paul squeals with excitement and delight. He never seems to be jealous and is so appreciative of everything Emily does for him. Oh, she loves him so! She often wonders why Paul is so sick. It doesn't seem fair, but she can never quite figure it out. So she decides to accept her feelings and live with things as they are and do the best she can. It helps us to pray and to read the Bible with Mom during their daily devotions. Emily especially likes Isaiah 40:28-31. (Read this passage to the children and mention that you will be looking at it more closely later.) She especially likes the part about the "eagles." It also helps to go out with Mom, Dad, or her new friend Tim, just to have fun.

Well, it is soon time for Emily, Dad, and Tim to go. As they leave, Dr. Jones comes in to see Paul, as he does every week now (use the clothespin figure). Mom and Dr. Jones are talking to each other as Emily, Dad, and Tim leave for the park.

"Yes, it's going to be a good day!" Emily thinks. "I wonder if Paul would like an ice cream cone for his present, or maybe I can make him a book with all the special things I find in the park pasted in it," she thinks, as she slips her hand into her dad's hand.

They walk happily to the park, with Tim running full speed ahead, chattering all the way.

"Yes, it's going to be a good day, for sure!"

Developing Activites

Coping Quilt[1] (25 minutes)

As you put the items back in the story box, allow the children time to discuss some of the feelings Emily had as she experienced Paul's illness (i.e., sadness, frustration, anger, less time with Mom and Dad, etc.) For most of the children, the story will be an unusual one. It will not be at

[1] Adapted from Joyce King and Carol Katzman, *Imagine That* (Glenview, IL: Scott, Foresman and Co., 1976).

all typical of their families, but it can be used as a spring-board for ideas, thoughts, and discussion. That is its purpose.

Be sure to emphasize how Emily and her family coped with illness. Talk about how they had good experiences and happy times during the crisis. Have the children name the things Emily did to help her feel better. The children may suggest such things as: Emily accepted her feelings, expressed her feelings, had time alone, wrote poetry, had special times with her brother Paul, read the Bible and prayed with her family, had fun times with her friend Tim, did fun things with her mom, dad, and Paul as a family, brought Paul a surprise present.

Provide colored construction paper squares (6 by 6 inches, 15.4 by 15.4 cm). As the children brainstorm, put the ideas on these precut papers. The children can do this, too. Then design a patchwork quilt using these idea squares. In the middle of the quilt put ''Isaiah 40:28-31.'' You might read the Bible passage for them again or remind them that you will be discussing the passage in more detail a bit later. Then pin all the idea squares side by side on a large bulletin board, or tape them together on the back side of the quilt and glue or tape the whole thing to a cardboard backing. Use heavy yarn, rickrack, or colored paper strips to outline each square of the quilt. As a finishing touch add lace or eyelet for the border.

Making a Banner (30 minutes)

Remind the children that one way of coping with an illness in the family is to turn to the Word of God. Allow the children to take a closer look at Isaiah 40:28-31. Read it together and help the children pick out the important words or phrases. It might be helpful to have the children write their own paraphrases. Take phrases from the passage and write them on a chalkboard or newsprint for all the children to see.

Provide burlap, felt, cloth, yarn, construction paper, dowel sticks, posterboard, glue, letter stencils, animals, nature items, figures of children, colored pens, paint, etc., for the children to make a poster or a banner. They may use their own thoughts or Bible verses (paraphrases or phrases). Encourage them to decorate their posters or banners with perhaps eagles, people running, clouds, birds, mountains, etc. You may also suggest that the children work together in small groups of two or three to create their projects. Allow the children time to work on them. When they have finished, allow them to share their work with the total group and perhaps hang their posters or banners around the room.

Closing Prayer (5 minutes)

When the children have finished their projects and hung them, invite them to come together again as a group. Guide the children in a prayer for all of their families. Thank God for each family, and also pray that God would help especially those families where there is sickness. You might wish to invite children to pray for those who are sick in their families. End by praising God for taking care of all of us, not only when we are sick, but also when we are well.

Bible Used in This Session: Isaiah 40:28-31

Partners in Mission

by Arline J. Ban

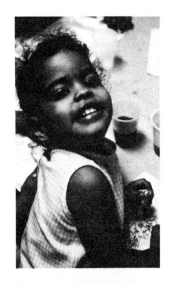
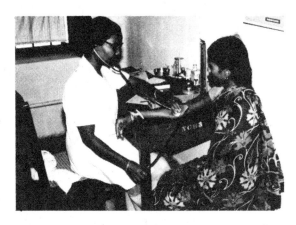

Unit Introduction

For too long, the role of the child within the Christian community has been viewed as one of observing and waiting to be "grown up" enough to be accepted and to participate fully in the life of the congregation!

This unit focuses on the child being seen as and accepted as a responsible person within the local church. Learning activities that involve a one-to-one relationship between adults and children are planned. The purpose of this approach is to help the children see themselves as partners with adults in taking a significant role in carrying on the mission of the local church.

What is partnership in mission? Partnership indicates shared experiences, mutual growing, nurturing, and partic-ipation which allows each person to make a significant contribution. In partnership there is need for trusting and enjoying each other, as well as that important feeling of "Hey, we are in this together!"

Growing Partnership

Partnership will not develop in one session! It does take time to grow. Adults who will participate in this unit, which uses a partnership approach, need to be chosen carefully for their understanding of children and for their flexibility as well as their availability to work with children between session times. In Session 1 a matching-word exercise is suggested for the purpose of pairing adults with children. You may feel that it is important to match partners before the first session in order to meet the needs of some children.

71

There may be children who need a particular male or female friend, or a grandparent figure. Distance may be another factor in selecting partners ahead of time. An adult who lives close to a child may be able to spend more time developing a relationship and become more involved by taking the child on field trips related to the mission activities of the church.

Adult partners need to take on the role of enabler and encourager with a willingness to develop teamwork. Children will also at times take on the role of enabler and encourager. But most of all, the adults who share in this unit must be able to take into consideration the perspective and abilities of the children when forming their expectations.

What does mission mean to children? Children begin to view it from their own realm of experience. The younger children in your group may see mission as following Jesus' way by helping others. They can see how expressing love to neighbors and providing various kinds of help to people in the community is doing what Jesus wanted us to do. We will guide growth in the meaning of mission by helping children to understand how people in other communities and other cultures live. Older children are becoming aware of a larger world. When they recognize that people everywhere have similar experiences and are able to identify with the problems of people in other countries, they begin to grasp the concept of worldwide mission. They can understand the need for others to know God's love through Christ.

To understand their own part in mission, children themselves need to *experience* giving for others. As they call on shut-ins, work for missionary projects, or make contact through letters with missionaries and with boys and girls who live on mission fields, they come closer to a firsthand experience of sharing in being missionaries themselves. They grow in their understanding of what it means to be or to become a Christian.

Children do have abilities to do mission work. Stories about children who served God have come down from the earlier days of Hebrew history. In Session 3 the story of Samuel is used to communicate how God trusts and values children and chooses to work through them. The story of the little Hebrew girl helping Naaman, which is used in Session 3, calls attention to the gifts of being sensitive to others and being willing to help others. The Scripture reference to the Great Commission in Session 2 is studied from the view of how children might see present-day disciples carrying out this mission. "Let Us Love One Another," used in Session 1, is related to the ways people in the Christian church act out their love.

Planning Ahead

Participating adults will need to be contacted well ahead of time to ensure working partnerships in this unit. It will be helpful to go through each session plan carefully. Share the purpose of the unit and of each session as you talk with the adults. Try to give an overview of what might happen in this unit. Allow brainstorming in order to discover some worthwhile mission activities that fit your situation. Do explore what the children will bring to the learning experience, i.e., their needs, their abilities, their understandings. Stress the importance of "being there and being counted on" by the child partners. Think through ways to listen actively and enable children to share significantly in these experiences.

This unit is planned in such a way that a one-to-one adult-child working/learning relationship is essential. If this is not possible in your situation, try an alternate plan of inviting a committee of adults to join a committee of children to explore ways of working together in the local church's missionary projects. Or the children themselves may identify a local need and then ask adults for their assistance. An example of local mission projects is to provide a program for "latchkey" children who need supervision after school or on days off from school. Another is to try to persuade the town or neighborhood council to provide adequate recreational programs and facilities for children.

Children may initiate a new project and need adult help with specific tasks that are involved in it. For example, the children might decide to send needed items to a program in Haiti for mentally retarded children. In Haiti at the College Pratique du Nord, a center for mentally retarded children has recently been started. The children range in age from ten to sixteen years. Since it is a new program, equipment is sorely needed. Suggested items to send to the center are: easy handwork, large sturdy puzzles, matching cards, simple toys. Wrap packages securely and send via parcel post to:

> College Pratique du Nord
> P.O. Box 11
> Cap Haitien, HAITI
> WEST INDIES

Mark on the parcel: "GIFT PARCEL." Declare its value at a very nominal cost.

Adult helpers will be needed to buy wood and use saws to make puzzles.

Resources for This Unit

- *Mission Service Projects* LS15-209 ($1.00)
  Judson Book Stores
  P.O. Box 851
  Valley Forge, PA 19482-0851

  or

  1505 Dundee Ave.
  Elgin, IL 60120

- UNICEF
  331 East 38th St.
  New York, NY 10016

● Filmstrip: "Proclaiming the Word"

This filmstrip is an overview of mission around the world. It has a special script for use with children. It includes a 10-minute audiocassette. Baptist references in the script can be deleted or changed when the script is used by other denominations. It may be purchased for $7.50, plus $1.25 for postage and handling, from American Baptist Films, P.O. Box 851, Valley Forge, PA 19482-0851; or Box 23204, Oakland, CA 94623.

Materials to Have Ready

You probably have readily available such items as pencils, paper, scissors, Bibles. Before the first session of this unit, you may want to gather other certain specific items.

Session 1: ● colored construction paper
● felt markers
● glue
● magazines
● yarn and string

● 2 boxes (or bags)
● marble (or penny)
● newsprint

Session 2: ● newsprint
● invite a missionary to come and talk about his or her work

Session 3: ● newsprint
● map or globe
● resource book giving information about the country chosen for mission project
● pictures of country
● newspaper articles about country
● bulletin board or wall for displaying pictures and articles
● write ahead for information on the Heifer Project, CROP, and UNICEF

Session 4: ● newsprint
● materials for stick or bag puppets (alternate activity)

Session 1

Find a Partner

Purpose

- To help children experience belonging in a community with adults.
- To help each child become acquainted with one adult with whom she or he may become a partner in the mission of the local church.

Background for Leader(s)

The most important thing that can happen in this session is for each child to feel good about himself or herself in a setting that involves sharing experiences with adults. To be affirmed as a person of worth within the Christian community is basic to being able to do mission work for others. As you look forward to this session, consider how the children feel about themselves as a part of your church. Are they often involved with adults in occasions of worship, fellowship dinners, work projects, intergenerational study? If so, they may respond readily to the idea of having an adult partner in this unit. However, they may still need encouragement to take responsibility for what happens when they are with adults.

It may be that the children in your group are more isolated from others in your church. Some may only take part in this particular program and not be involved in other local church happenings. The presence of adults may puzzle them or threaten them. They may take a little more time accepting individual adults and feeling comfortable with the idea of working in a one-to-one partnership with an adult.

The beginning activity can help new adult-child partners to learn something about each other. The ''Find a Partner'' activity is one way to form child-adult partner teams. If there is a need to choose adult-child partners ahead of time (see unit introduction), this activity may be eliminated. The word parts could be handed out to the appropriate partners. Talking about ''how people in my church show love to each other'' is an exercise to help children and adults recognize ways in which love is expressed in the community. It has the potential for allowing children to recognize ways in which followers of Jesus belong to each other. Be aware and accepting of the simple, real ways in which children see love being expressed. Seeing people respect each other and care for each other in day-to-day struggles is indeed a real demonstration of Christian love.

A Checklist for Getting Ready

- Gather a variety of materials to create story tags.
- Prepare slips and boxes for half-words.
- Print words of song on newsprint.

Beginning Activities

Make Story Tags (10-15 minutes)

Greet the children and adults as they arrive. Suggest that each person create a story tag about his or her life. Encourage everyone to picture in his or her story such things as what my family is like, what I like to eat, what I like to do best, and so on. Ask the young people to print their first names in large, bold letters on the tag so that they can be seen easily by others. Magazine pictures, yarn pictures, or stick figures can be used to illustrate the tags. Prepare a large working space, making available a variety of materials such as colored construction paper, white paper, crayons, colored felt markers, scissors, glue, magazines, yarn and

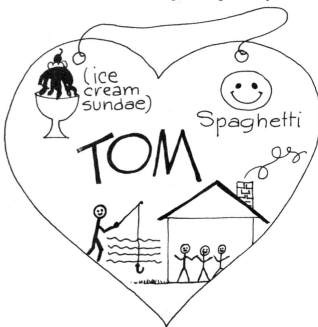

pieces of string for persons to use as they make their story tags. The paper for the tags needs to be at least 9 by 12 inches (23.1 by 30.8 cm) and may be cut in any shape or design the person chooses. String or yarn can be attached to the tags so they can be hung around the neck.

Find a Partner (5-10 minutes)

When each person has finished making a story tag, suggest that he or she find a partner by matching parts of a word. Here is how it may be done:

Prepare two boxes (or bags) which contain slips of paper with half a word written on them. One box will contain the slips of paper on which the first half of the words are written. The other box will contain the papers on which the second half of the words are written. Suggest that the adults draw their slips from one box and the children draw theirs from the other box. An adult and child who match slips and complete a word become partners. Use words that relate to the theme of the unit, "Partners in Mission." Choose from the following words according to the number in your group.

work   plan   worship

play   serve

love   talk

study   pray   partners

sign   help   mission

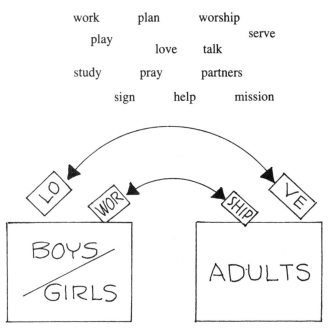

Conversation with a Partner (5-10 minutes)

When partners have been matched, forming partner-teams, encourage them to get acquainted with each other by sharing the drawings, pictures, or decorations on their story tags. Then suggest that each pair talk about their word and how it helps the people in your church to do all the activities in which they are involved.

Developing Activities

Get Together in a Circle (10-15 minutes)

Give a special welcome to the adult participants at this time. Explain to the boys and girls that the adults are not guests but are joining with the group to discover the ways adults and children can share in helping other people to know God's love. Make clear to the children that they will actually be doing the activities in the next few sessions with their adult partners.

To help everyone become acquainted, suggest that each child introduce his or her partner by name and tell one thing about the partner's story tag. The adult partner will then tell in one sentence (simply please!) what their matching word is and how it relates to the life of the church. For example: "*Work* is our word. The people in our church work in many ways—serving together on committees, keeping the building clean, teaching and collecting money to help others." Or, another example: "Our word is *play*. The people in our church enjoy each other in times of play, such as picnics, church suppers, and so on."

Play a Game (10 minutes)

Play the following game to get to know each other better.

"Marble, Marble, How You Wander!"

The group stands in a circle and passes a marble (or a penny) from one to the other. "It" stands in the center of the circle and tries to guess which player has the object in his or her hand. "It" has as many guesses as are needed to catch the passer. The following chant is said while passing the item:

Marble, marble how you wander . . .
From one hand to the other.
Is it fair? Is it fair?
To keep poor (*name of "It"*) standing there.

The person who is caught with the marble in his or her hand or drops it, changes places with "It."

Practice passing the marble and chanting the rhyme before the game begins. A good way to pass the marble so it is not easily seen, is to hold the object in one fist with palm down, and then drop it into the upraised palm of the next person. ·

"It" should stand with eyes closed through ten counts to give the players a chance to start the marble around. Be aware of frustrating any individual who is "It." If after a short while, "It" fails to catch the marble passer, suggest that someone else in the circle volunteer to take a turn at being "It." Spend enough time for the group to feel good about playing, but not too much time to bore the children. Encourage just having fun together rather than competition between the players.

Talking It Over (10-15 minutes)

Divide the group into smaller groups of six or three sets of partners. Suggest that each group read 1 John 4:7 and then discuss the answer to the question, "How do the people in my church show love to one another?" Ask each group to list their ideas on a sheet of newsprint to share with the entire group. One person can be chosen to record ideas and another to report to the whole group. Some of the ideas that are suggested might be: Taking care of each other when there is trouble or sickness . . . helping people to have friends . . . enjoying each other . . . giving rides to people going to church.

Closing Activities (10 minutes)

Gather everyone together. Refer to the teachings of Jesus, who taught us to love one another. Ask the groups to share their lists of ways people love each other. Post the newsprint lists side by side on the wall for all to see.

Sing the following words to the hymn tune "St. Peter C.M." (used with "In Christ There Is No East or West"). If the children are not familiar with the tune, play it through for them and then say the words together before singing them.

We are the ones who do Christ's work
In mission everywhere.
Both young and old are partners here
We give, we serve, we care.
—words by Virginia Sargent

Close with a prayer of thanksgiving for all the people who share love with others in the home, the neighborhood, and the world.

As each person leaves this session, have him or her pin the story tags to a bulletin board or tape them to a large sheet of paper over which the title "PARTNERS" is printed.

Bible Used in This Session: 1 John 4:7

Session 2

What Is Mission?

Purpose
- To help children and adults understand Jesus' call to mission.
- To help children become aware of how they may share as partners in the mission of the local church.

Background for Leader(s)

In Matthew 28:16-20 we have the record of the experience of the disciples with the risen Christ. In the Great Commission they are challenged, and through them the church in every generation, with the mission of Christ. The message and ministry of Jesus are to be taken to the ends of the earth. The disciples are told to follow the example of Jesus and to do God's will. Jesus promises to be with his disciples always. In this session the children and adults will explore these verses together to come to an understanding of what is mission. Be aware that some children may not have been baptized or may not have observed the act of baptism, and therefore will be unlikely to understand its meaning. Allow room for the children to discuss their questions as you study these verses. The exercise of rewriting the verses is a way to check how children perceive meaning for their own lives in our day. Guide them in using their own words to express what they think the verse means. To some it may mean: "Be my helpers and teach all people how to love each other." Adult partners need to share in the wording, but to emphasize the way a child would explain the words of Jesus.

Children learn best by actually doing. So learning activities are provided to allow children to plan how they can find out information about missionary activity and how they might participate in the mission of their own local church. Specific plans for partners to gather information are to be made in this session.

A Checklist for Getting Ready
- Print the directions for the beginning activity on a newsprint sheet or a chalkboard.
- Prepare to tell the story of William Carey, "An Adventurer for Christ."
- Print the stanza of "In Christ There Is No East or West" on newsprint.

Developing Activities

Discover: What Is Mission? (10-15 minutes)

Suggest that the partners chosen in the last session get together and begin to work on the first activity.
(Print the following directions on a newsprint chart or on a chalkboard for all to see and to guide the Bible study of the partner-teams.)

> BE A BIBLE INVESTIGATOR . . .
>   DISCOVER THE ANSWERS . . .
> Jesus gave his disciples a mission —
>   A SPECIAL TASK!!

Find Out: What mission did Jesus give to or ask of his disciples?

Read: Matthew 28:19-20 (A TEV [*Good News*] edition or *The New English Bible* will be clearer to the children.)

Think About:
- What did Jesus want his disciples to do?
- Where were they to go?
- What four things did he ask them to do?
- How do followers of Jesus continue to do this mission today?
- How would you put what Jesus said to his disciples in your own words?

Rewrite the Verse as if Jesus were talking directly to us today. How might the "special task" be worded? What would Jesus tell us today?

Then write your verse on newsprint to share with others. (Provide another sheet of newsprint for the rewritten verses.)

Thinking About Missions (10-15 minutes)

Gather the group together. Ask the partner-teams to share what they discovered in their Bible study. What did they find to be the "special task" Jesus gave to his disciples? Refer briefly to the rewriting of the verses and compare their similarities. Mention that today we know about Jesus and God's love for us because Jesus' followers down through the ages have carried out Jesus' mission.

Share a Story (5-10 minutes)

William Carey— An Adventurer for Christ!

William Carey grew up in an exciting time! So many

new things were happening in the world. The newspapers told such things as: "The colonies in the New World want independence!" "Captain Cook discovers the Pacific Islands!" Even though he lived in a small town in England, William's world was getting bigger and bigger every day.

As a boy William Carey dreamed: "Oh, how I would love to sail on those ships and travel on the seas! I wonder what it would be like to discover other countries and to see how different people live?" He loved adventure, and read all he could about the new trade routes among countries around the world. He was especially interested in the lands and people in the Far East and India.

As a grown man William Carey continued to think about faraway places and the people who lived around the world. He became pastor of a Baptist church. The church could only pay him a little money, so he worked as a shoemaker making leather boots to earn extra money. Whenever he found time, he studied languages such as Latin, Greek, and Hebrew. He also studied hard to understand the Bible.

One day Carey took his bag full of leather boots to sell to his employer, Mr. Gotch. That day, Mr. Gotch had a bit of a twinkle in his eye. "Mr. Carey, I understand that you are studying several languages." "Yes, sir!" replied William Carey. "How much do you earn selling boots?" When Carey told him, Mr. Gotch hesitated and with a smile said, "Mr. Carey, there is no need for you to go on spoiling my leather by making boots. I will pay you ten shillings a week to get on as fast as you can with your Latin, Hebrew, and Greek." Mr. Gotch knew that William Carey had special gifts as a student and helped him in this way.

William Carey studied Matthew 28:19-20 very seriously. He thought about it for a long time and decided that Jesus' commission was not only for the first disciples but for Christians in his time as well.

Carey tried to persuade English Baptists: "We must send people as missionaries to other parts of the world, so they can know Jesus and his teachings!" Again and again, the people said, "No! Those people may hurt us! They do not understand our ways! If God wants them to know about Jesus, God will take care of it!" Carey did not give up. In 1792 he persuaded them to organize a missionary society for the purposes of sending missionaries to other countries. William Carey himself became their first missionary to India.

It was not easy for Carey and his family to be missionaries. In India they suffered in many ways. They were poor, they often became ill, and one of their children died. William Carey would not give up, even though the people were against him. He spent forty-one years as a missionary in India. During that time he translated the Bible into many languages and worked in other ways to help the people live better.

William Carey was not afraid to try new ways of doing things that would help missionaries be able to go into all the world to preach and teach as Jesus commanded.

Finding Out About Missions (5-10 minutes)

Refer to how Christians today continue to work in missions as Jesus has asked us to do. Guide the children in recognizing what they already know about the ways Christians help others. Discuss what they understand and know about mission work as you attempt to answer the following questions: "What are the ways Christians today continue to carry out Jesus' mission?" "How does our church work in missions?" List the ideas on newsprint.

Suggest that all people in the church—children, young people, and adults—can work together in missions. Point out that, in order to find the ways we can help, we need to investigate all the ways our church works in mission.

Ask the group to think as if they were investigators searching to find out about missions. Where would they go for information? Who could help them? What questions could they ask? Encourage their ideas. Ask a partner-team to list on newsprint the ideas as they are mentioned in the group discussion.

The newsprint chart might look something like this:

Investigating My Church's Mission

WHO?	WHAT?
Our Minister	Ask: How does our church carry out Jesus' mission? How do we help people outside the church family know about Jesus? Who are the church members who work in the community? How do they work? What can we do to help them?
Member of the Mission Committee	Do we support a certain mission or missionary? Where? Who? How? What can we do to share in missionary work here in our own community? How can we help in missions in our country? In our world? What project can we share in?
Member of the Finance Committee	Where does money that we give for mission go? How do we raise money?
Member of the Committee on Social Concerns	How are the members in our church responsible for people who have special needs? (retarded persons? persons with disabilities? older adults? refugees? persons in hospitals? prisoners? people who need food/clothing?) What can we do to help?

Member of the
Building Committee

How is our church building used for mission work? What groups do we allow to use the building during the week as a way of mission service to them? What could we do?

Plan: Who will find out?

Look over the list of possible ways to find out information and then ask each of the partner-teams to choose one of the persons to interview. If your group is large, two or three partner-teams may choose to work together interviewing the same person. Each team will then spend time to plan the details of the interview, such as:

- When shall we interview? (Interviewing will probably need to be done between group sessions because of the amount of time involved.)
- Who will call and make arrangements for us to talk with the person?
- What questions will we ask? What specific information do we want?
- How will we take notes? Who will be responsible for taking notes? (Some may choose to use a tape recorder to tape the interview.)

Alternate Suggestions

You may choose to invite one or more persons repre-senting one of the above committees to this session to be interviewed by the children and adults. If so, contact them ahead of time and ask that they be ready to suggest realistic possibilities for ways children can participate in mission. They will keep in mind the children's abilities as well as their time limits.

Invite a missionary to come and share the experiences of his or her work with the group. There may be a home missionary or an international missionary in your area who could tell firsthand about mission work. Contact your denominational office for information about missionaries who may be available for this session. Ask the visitor to bring slides or a film about the mission work that would be suitable for children.

Closing Activities (10 minutes)

Ask partner-teams to share the plans they have made.

Sing the words to the hymn "In Christ There Is No East or West." Then sing together the stanza found in Session 1. Before singing, read the words together and discuss their meaning.

Close with a prayer of thanksgiving for all who have gone into the world to spread the message of Jesus.

Bible Used in This Session: Matthew 28:16-20

William Carey

Session 3

What Shall We Do Now?

Purpose

- To help children plan ways to share in mission activity.

Background for Leader(s)

In this session, the partner-teams will begin to learn about the meaning of missions through "doing" mission. Children and adults will spend time in reviewing the many possibilities for ways they can serve in partnership together. The participation of children in considering the use of their abilities and making a choice of what they can do to help in mission activity is an important part of the session. Steps are provided for decision making. Children want to feel they are sharing with adults in the planning. The adult partners need to recognize the gifts children can bring to the actual work of missions. They will also help in enabling realistic expectations in the planning.

The important element in this experience is *doing it together*. Some of the plans cannot be completed in one or two sessions. It is possible that the mission activity will continue over a long period of time and involve an ongoing relationship between adult and child.

Possibilities for mission are suggested to help stimulate your thinking about the many ways to become involved in international missions, national missions, or in community concerns.

The story of Samuel (1 Samuel 3:10-18) is used to call our attention to the ways God works through people and particularly through children.

A Checklist for Getting Ready

- Prepare the charts for reporting in the beginning activity.

Developing Activities

Partner-Teams Chart Findings (10-15 minutes)

When they arrive, partner-teams are to jot down their findings about how the local church is involved in missions and the ways children may share in that mission. They need only to use words or brief phrases to report what they have discovered.

Provide two wall charts (newsprint) for the reporting. On one chart place the title "What Our Church Is Doing in Missions." On the other chart, place the title "What We Can Do in Missions." Over the charts, place the words: OUR MISSION

Our Mission

Reporting on Missions (10-15 minutes)

When all have had a chance to record their discoveries, gather the group together in a circle around the charts. Give each partner-team a turn to explain what they found out.

Checking Out the Possibilities (10-15 minutes)

Discuss how the group would like to share in mission projects. Refer to the chart "What We Can Do." Talk over the answers to the following questions:

- What additional ideas do we have about these suggestions?
- Are there other projects we might do?

Check or list those suggestions the group would like to work on. Then talk over the answers to the following questions:

- What abilities do we have which enable us to work on one or more of these projects? Which projects could we do well?
- What special equipment or materials would we need?
- Where could we get what we need?

- Whom would we need to help us?
- Will we need transportation? Whom could we ask to help us?
- Would some projects take too much time to do?
- What is possible for us to do? What is not possible?

Place a check beside the projects that are possibilities and decide which one or ones the group will work on. Suggest that each partner-team may want to choose a project or join with other teams in working on a project. The mission activity does not necessarily have to be completed within the sessions of this unit. A realistic time limit will need to be set for working on some projects. Suggest that at least one group work on a project related to international missions and another to meeting the needs in the nearby community.

Working on Projects (25-35 minutes)

The partner-teams will begin to work on the projects they have chosen. They need first to plan a step-by-step procedure of how to do the project, gather material, make assignments, and so on. Most projects will require activity between sessions, so careful plans will need to be made to follow through with the activity.

The following are suggested ways children and adults might participate together in mission. These ideas may supplement the thinking, deciding, and planning of the group in your own situation.

Participate in Supporting a National Mission

1. Survey the needs in your own community or area. How could you serve in Christian centers, in refugee programs, or with a different ethnic group or economic class? Take field trips to visit centers to see at first hand how mission helps people in need. Sources of information are your pastor and local or area denominational offices.
2. Provide a caring ministry in homes and hospitals. In North America there are many retirement homes, children's homes, and organizations that provide special services to children because Christians working through the churches make the work possible. Contact those homes in your area to see how partner-teams can respond with practical ways of ministry. Community social agencies may be able to suggest nursing homes and hospitals where projects are welcome.

Prepare a music program, a worship program, a drama, or a party to present to persons confined to a home.

Participate in Supporting an International Mission

1. Find out about the mission.
   - Locate it on a world map or globe.
   - Learn something about the culture: How do people live, work, play, study? What do they like to eat? How do they dress? How is their culture similar to ours; how is it different?
   - What time zone are they in? What time is it for us when they eat, sleep, work, go to school, etc?
2. Plan to contact the missionary (or missionaries) you are supporting.
   - Write a letter to find out about the work of the mission field. You might:
   —Ask for names of children who could be pen pals.
   —Ask for ways children together with adults can help in the work of the mission, such as collecting clothes, books, or money for a specific need.
   —Find out a suggested time when your partner-team can pray for the mission work, which would be the same time the persons on the mission field are praying for you.
   - Send snapshots of your team or group with the letter.
3. Help publicize the mission work of your church. Encourage others to share in the work. Plan for a bulletin board display in a location where the people in your church will see it. Some things to put in the display are:
   - A world map locating the mission station.
   - Pictures of the country and the mission station. These may come from the missionaries, geographic or travel magazines, newspaper articles, denominational magazines, newsletters.
   - Recent letters from the missionaries.
   - A list of specific items or ways to help that have been suggested by the missionaries or your church's mission committee.
   - A request to remember the missionaries (include the names) in prayer.

Participate in Supporting Our Community

Adopt persons to whom you will give special attention through:

—visiting regularly
—sending cards on holidays and birthdays
—making scrapbooks about: ''What my church is doing'' to share with these persons
—help decorate the person's room for Christmas
—share home-baked cookies and cakes
—tape the story of the person's life

Special Help Projects

Organizations in many communities are banding together to form food banks and clothing depots for the unemployed and the poor. Check out the newspapers for special requests to help others in need. Partners in mission can help in many ways through earning money, collecting items, and publicizing the need in church bulletins and on posters so others are aware of the ways they might share.

Some World Service Projects are:

The Heifer Project International, P.O. Box 808, Little

Rock, AR 72203. They will send free materials on sending chicks, rabbits, pigs, sheep, goats, bees, and heifers to help deprived people help themselves.

CROP is a project sponsored by Church World Service, P.O. Box 968, Elkhart, Indiana 46514, for world hunger. Special materials are available for projects with children.

UNICEF. Write U.S. Committee for UNICEF, 331 E. 38th St., New York, NY 10016 for information about the water project.

Closing Activities (5-10 minutes)

Gather the group together from their various activities. Mention that at the beginning of the next session partner-teams may continue to work on their mission projects.

Share the following story about the boy Samuel, who was counted on by God to do God's work.

Long before the time of Jesus, a young boy named Samuel was taken to the temple at Shiloh to work with the priest Eli. Samuel's mother, Hannah, told Eli: "I promised God that if I had a son, I would give him up to do God's work." Samuel liked being at the temple and working with Eli. One night God came to Samuel and gave the young boy an important message. God was judging Eli's family because they had done things that God did not like. When Samuel told Eli everything that God said to him, Eli knew that Samuel had been chosen to be a leader of God's people. God was with Samuel as he grew up. The people trusted Samuel and honored him as a man who spoke for God.

Close with a prayer for persons you have come to know who are working in mission activities. Name them, if possible.

Bible Used in This Session: 1 Samuel 3:10-18

Session 4

To Be Continued . . .

Purpose

- To continue working as partners in mission activity.
- To guide awareness of the children to the practical ways each person can continue to be responsible for contributing to the mission of the local church.

Background for Leader(s)

It is important, in this final session of the unit, that participants recognize the work of missions in the local church as an ongoing activity in the life of the Christian community. Time will be provided to finish or continue to work on any mission project activity that is possible within the session. Evaluation can be a learning activity as partners and the group as a whole think over what they have done and what they have learned. The adults will want to share positively in the evaluation time. Affirm what has been done. Mention specific ways children have helped and contributed. Encourage reflection by looking objectively at what could have been done better or easier. This needs to be done without putting down or threatening any individual. A suggestion for doing this is: "Next time, we might do it this way. . . ." Be aware that when children feel free to express what they think and feel, they do have good ideas to contribute.

There are many lessons to be learned from the Scripture reference to the Hebrew servant girl (2 Kings 5:1-14). The main emphasis important for this session is on how the girl helped where she was with what she knew from her own experience. This story can help guide the group's thinking about how we participate with others in mission projects and also ways each person can continue to be aware of the needs of others. We can learn how to be responsible by serving God in everyday life.

It is hoped that by the end of this unit, child-adult partners will have been able to develop a long-term relationship and will continue working in mission activity. It is hoped, too, that these sessions have enabled the child-adult teams to live day to day as loving and helping persons following Jesus' teachings and example.

A Checklist for Getting Ready

- Prepare to tell the story of "The Little Hebrew Girl."
- Make a chart or reproduce individual copies of "Things I Can Be Responsible For," page 85.

Developing Activities

Continue Working on Projects (20-35 minutes)

Greet members of the group as they arrive and suggest that partner-teams continue to work on their mission projects. Those who cannot work on their particular projects during this time, may choose one of the alternate activities.

Share Progress and Evaluate (15 minutes)

Talk over the progress of the various mission projects.

- What has been completed?
- What have we yet to do?
- What project activities will we continue?

Then, as a way of enabling partners to evaluate what they have done, talk over the following:

- What has gone well?
- What did you like?
- What could we have done better? If we were going to do it over again, what would we do differently?
- What new ideas came to you about the needs of other people in the world?
- What are some ways we can continue to share in our church's work in missions?

Story of the Little Hebrew Girl (5 minutes)

The little Hebrew girl could have been very mean! After all, she had been carried away as a captive by the great Captain Naaman. "Here I am in the land of Syria," she thought. "I am so far away from the people I know and love. Who could have guessed that I would end up being a servant girl to Captain Naaman's wife? I am glad she is kind to me. I only wish that she were happier. She seems so sad."

One day the girl found her mistress crying very hard. "How can I help her?" thought the little girl. Then she found out that Naaman had a very serious skin disease. No one knew how to cure it. Naaman would have to go away and live alone until he died. The Hebrew girl remembered the land she came from. She remembered the wise man her people called Elisha. He was a prophet who spoke for God and could help people. One day she said to her mistress: "I wish that Captain Naaman would go to the prophet in Samaria. Elisha will know how to cure him!" Captain

Naaman's wife told her husband what the servant girl suggested. Naaman in turn talked with the king. They decided that he should go to Samaria and find the prophet. So Naaman set out with lots of gifts for Elisha just in case he could cure him. When he reached Elisha's home a servant came out and told him: "Elisha says to go and wash seven times in the river Jordan." Naaman was angry! "What a silly thing to tell me to do!" he thought. "Elisha could at least have come out of his house to look at me, to touch me, and pray to his God for me!" But his servants urged him: "If Elisha himself had told you to do something difficult, you would have done it. Why not do what the servant says. Wash yourself and see if you can be cured." So Naaman went down to the river and dipped himself seven

times as Elisha told him to do, and he was cured. He was so happy that he presented Elisha with all the gifts he had brought. Elisha refused the gifts, saying, "I cannot accept gifts for doing my job as a servant of God." Naaman was so impressed with Elisha that he came to believe in the God Elisha served.

Naaman returned to Syria cured of his disease. His king, his wife, and his friends were all happy for him. But most of all, the little Hebrew girl was glad that she had helped Naaman to be cured!

Things I Can Be Responsible For . . .
(15 minutes)

Discuss the story briefly. Ask how the little Hebrew girl

served God. For a few moments talk about the ways we can serve God as we go about doing things at home, at school, and in the community.

Place the following checklist on newsprint or reproduce it so that each person in your group has a copy to keep. Suggest that everyone read and think about the list for a few moments in silence and then get together with his or her partner and talk over ways each person can continue sharing in missions.

Encourage everyone to choose at least one thing he or she promises to do. Urge group members to add other ideas to those listed. Also stress the need to be realistic about what is possible to do. The partners might talk over how they will continue to share with each other in mission activity or to be in touch with each other to share their progress on the chosen responsibility.

Things I Can Be Responsible For

____ Pray regularly for (*a specific missionary or mission project, or world need*).

____ Look through my closet and find some things I am willing to share with someone who needs them.

____ Save from my allowance regularly to give to my church for mission work.

____ Collect newspapers or returnable bottles and sell them. Use the money to give to a specific mission project of my church.

____ Shovel snow or cut grass for some person who has been ill or who is elderly.

____ Invite a newcomer to my neighborhood, or someone who does not belong to a church, to go with me to church activities.

____ Adopt a grandparent. Choose an older person who has no grandchildren—or who lives far away from family members. Pay special attention to the adopted grandparent and plan to do things with him or her.

____ Plan to involve a shut-in in a project to help others, such as making gifts for hospital trays or making get-well cards.

____ Write to a missionary or a child who lives in another country.

____ What other ways can I think of to take part in mission?

Alternate Activities

If time in the beginning of this session is not needed by some partner-teams to work on mission projects, encourage them to choose one of the following activities:

1. Write prayers for specific missionaries or mission projects. These may be written on sheets of newsprint to share with the entire group in the closing moments of this session. They could also be shared with the gathered congregation in corporate worship.

The prayers could be printed in church bulletins or newsletters. Copies of the prayers may also be sent to the missionaries.

2. Illustrate the words to the hymn, "In Christ There Is No East or West," that have been used in these sessions. A wall chart or mural might be created to illustrate how the local church works in missions around the world.

3. Dramatize the story of "The Little Hebrew Girl" (2 Kings 5:1-14). Read the story and plan how it might be presented dramatically. Children and adults might take the roles of those in the story and act it out spontaneously as they fit into the character parts. Others may choose to recreate the story through the use of simple stick puppets or bag puppets. Urge the persons taking the character parts to put the conversation and the happenings into their own words.

4. Create parallel charts to the Great Commission (Matthew 28:19-20). Write the words of Jesus on one newsprint chart. Illustrations of how Jesus ministered can be sketched under the words. On the chart which is parallel to the words of Jesus cut out pictures or words taken from newspapers and current news magazines that tell of the many kinds of needs in our world (for example, peace, war, nuclear threat, hunger, cure for cancer . . .) Another chart may show the good works that are being done. Your charts might include things like this:

Go into all the world...	starvation in Africa People without homes Threat of War	Disabled go on tour of Museum Meals on wheels Big Sister program begins

Closing Activities (5-10 minutes)

Gather everyone together and sing the verse to "In Christ There Is No East or West," which was sung in the previous sessions. Close with a prayer of thanksgiving for each child present (name each child in prayer) and ask for God's guidance as each continues to grow in the understanding of God and how to serve God.

> **Bible Used in This Session**: 2 Kings 5:1-14; Matthew 28:19-20

Sharing, Saving, Spending

by Joy Shih Ng

Unit Introduction

Talk about money, and most of us cringe or have an anxiety attack. Emotions of some kind usually come into the picture when money is discussed. We may have visions of bills floating in doors, windows, and every conceivable crack in the house. We hurt when a paycheck is cashed and the dollars are quickly gobbled up by the cash register at a grocery store. We are frustrated when we spend a lot of cash and come home with only a small bag of necessities. We dream of eating out at a fancy restaurant when in reality the most we can afford is a family outing to the local ice cream parlor. We're angry when we finish paying the car loan and then the car falls apart. We are envious as we sit in our home with freezing temperatures outside and think about our neighbors vacationing in the Bahamas.

No doubt about it, money plays a vital part in our lives. Whether we earn it or it is given to us, we share it, we save it, and more often than not, we spend it. Money brings happiness, we are told, and it carries clout. ''Money talks'' and ''We're in the money'' are expressions we hear often. Americans tend to judge one another, as well as the rest of the world, by the amount of money they have in their bank accounts. This is evident by the way we talk, the company we keep, the clothes we wear, the neighborhood we live in, the schools we attend.

Some people believe that the super-rich and the super-poor have one thing in common: Neither worries about money. One group has so much money that it is unnecessary to worry. The other group has so little money that it never even becomes a part of their lives. There are others who would say that, to those with so little, the money or lack of it becomes *very* significant. But most of us would fall into categories somewhere between the two extremes. Most of us worry about money, and we worry about it a lot.

As Christians we often try to live a lifestyle that exhibits freedom from worry and despair. The Bible says we are not to worry about life's necessities, because God will provide for them. Why then, do we have headaches when income tax time rolls around? Why do we agonize not over how many bills we have to pay but over which ones to pay first?

Because money has played an important role in the lives of people throughout history, we cannot deny its significance. Many times the courses of our lives are determined by money. We may wonder—if money plays such a significant role in our daily lives—in what ways is this affecting our children? What are our children learning about money—about the use and place of it in our lives?

In the four sessions of this unit, you and the children will be encouraged to think about money. Children will be discovering ways to gain money, exploring ways to share money, learning to be good stewards (or caretakers) by saving money, and practicing ways in which to spend money carefully and wisely.

It is hoped that, after taking part in the study and experiences provided in this unit, children will have a better understanding of the role of money in their lives. They will learn ways to begin implementing their faith by the use of their money and resources. Children can help us as adults to be reminded of the wonderful and plentiful resources entrusted to us by God. Perhaps one day we, too, may hear "Well done, good and faithful servant" (Matthew 25:21).

Materials to Have Ready

Session 1:
- situations printed on signs so all children can read them, or typed on cards—enough so that there are copies for every two or three students
- questions for discussion posted either on newsprint or on a chalkboard so that all children can see them
- all ingredients and equipment for making the cookies. (See the recipe on page 89.)
- new words to be sung to "Row, Row, Row Your Boat," on a chart so all of the children can read them

Session 2:
- legal-size letter envelopes (7 per child), hole puncher, thick colorful yarn
- self-adhesive bandages for each child

Session 3:
- manufacturers' cents-off coupons
- story about Benjamin Franklin (in Spencer Johnson, *The Value of Saving: The Story of Benjamin Franklin*. San Diego: Value Communications Inc., 1978) from your own library or a public library

- penny for a game to be played at the end of the session

Session 4:
- tape of several TV commercials advertising candy, toys, games, sugar-filled breakfast cereals, etc.
- various catalogues from department stores, discount houses, mail order houses, etc.

Resources for This Unit

Johnson, Spencer, *The Value of Saving, The Story of Benjamin Franklin*. San Diego: Value Communications, Inc., 1978.

Wilt, Joy, *A Kid's Guide to Managing Money*. Chicago: Children's Press, 1982.

In this book, in terms that children will understand, the author helps children to deal with the importance, the origins, and the uses of money. Children will be helped to realize and appreciate the value of money and how to use it wisely to enhance their lives and the lives of others. The book not only explains where money came from and why it exists today but suggests creative money-making projects to help the children earn money. Then guidelines are given for managing the earnings, such as saving, donating, and spending. This book is helpful in enabling children to understand that money, when it is obtained fairly and used properly, is a wonderful responsibility. It also teaches that everything we have comes to us as a gift from God. As we learn to earn and to manage money, we are learning to become good stewards of God's gifts. Learning lessons such as these will enable children to be better equipped to live healthy, exciting lives.

Wilt, Joy, *A Consumer's Guide for Kids*. Waco: Educational Products Division, Word, Inc.

The complex "push and pull" of today's economic system is looked at in this book in ways that children will understand. A growing number of children today become consumers at very early ages. This book helps them to see and understand how consumers are encouraged to buy and gives guidelines to follow when buying goods and/or services. It helps children to see that being a wise consumer is also a part of being good stewards of God's gifts to us. Learning these lessons will enable more fulfilling lives for our children.

The Gift That Lasts, a color motion picture, 18 minutes. Rental, $18.00, from American Baptist Films, Box 851, Valley Forge, PA 19482; or Box 23204, Oakland, CA 94623.

This film, based on a story by Pearl Buck and set in the Great Depression of the mid-1930s, is about a twelve-year-old boy who has only thirty-nine cents to buy a present for his dad. What the boy does provides his father with an experience never to be forgotten. The film, suitable for both children and adults, has a stewardship message appropriate for any time of the year.

Session 1

Gaining Money

Session Purposes

- To help children learn the value of money.
- To help children discover possible and appropriate ways to gain money.

Background for Leader(s)

Few people would dispute the fact that money is important in our society. Money is needed as a way to exchange skills, labor, talents, or goods. We cannot provide ourselves with all that we need today. So we work and/or produce in exchange for money which we then use to purchase goods, labor, and services of someone else. For instance, most of us cannot make our own shoes. We cannot provide our own heat or electricity without the help of someone else's product. We need money to meet our physical needs—to feed us, to clothe us, to provide shelter. Money is also useful in other ways. It can help us to do the things we want to do, to get the things we think we need. It can enable us to help others or to show them our appreciation. Money helps us toward achieving our goals in life.

In the past most children did not come into contact with money. Parents and guardians provided the necessities and the luxuries when they could afford them, without consulting the child. Today's children are in positions of having money and using it. They are given allowances. They are entrusted with carrying money to and from school. They run errands to the store and make their own choices when shopping for clothes and other items. More and more, pressure from peers and from television and magazine ads encourages children to be consumers, thus increasing their desire to obtain money or *more* money.

As you prepare for this session, study the passage on money as recorded in 1 Timothy 6:6-10 (TEV). Notice that it is not money that "is a source of all kinds of evil," rather, it is "the *love* of money." Herein lies the key, as the Scripture passage continues: "Some have been so eager to have [money] that they have wandered away from the faith and have broken their hearts with many sorrows." Throughout these four sessions it is hoped that leaders can begin to help children to see that difference between having money and loving it. It is our feelings about money and the place that we give to money that determines whether money is harmful or helpful to us.

Beginning Activities

Thinking About Allowances (15-20 minutes)

A common way that most children gain money is by receiving an allowance. You may want to discuss briefly how the children feel about allowances. How many do receive allowances? How many earn money? Be sensitive to children in your group who may not get allowances. It is important that what they have to say and how they feel is valued and understood. In this activity children will hear about life situations that deal with allowances and be given opportunities to discuss them.

Divide the group into two or three smaller groups, which will discuss each situation presented and report their solutions. If you have written out the situations on newsprint, post the first one and read it to the children. If you have typed it on cards, read it to the group and then give each group a card so that they will have the situation to refer to.

Allow time for the groups to discuss the situation and answer the questions related to each situation. The questions need to be on newsprint or on a chalkboard so that everyone can see them and refer to them as they participate in the discussion.

After the groups have discussed the questions for the first situation, allow some time for each group to tell how they felt or how they answered the questions. Then move on and follow the same process for situation 2 and situation 3. Do only as many situations as you can in about 15-20 minutes.

Situation 1: Allison gets $1 a week allowance. Bobby gets 75 cents a week. Bobby thinks he should get as much as Allison because they are the same age. What do you think?
Questions to think about: What do you need to know about each family? What do you need to know about each child in order to decide? What are some things Bobby may need to do to show that he can handle an increase in his allowance?

Situation 2: Tanika thinks she should get an increase in her allowance for making her own bed and helping with dinner. What do you think?
Questions to think about: Should payment for family responsibilities be included in an allowance? Talk about why you say "yes" or "no." Are there some chores for which family members need to get paid? What would they be? What are some other ways Tanika might earn more money?

Situation 3: Roberto spent all his allowance on a toy that broke right away. His Mom says if he continues to buy things foolishly she'll take away his allowance. What do you think?

Questions to think about: Is an allowance your *own* money to spend as you wish? Why do you say "yes" or "no"? Would you punish Roberto? If so, how? What lesson can Roberto learn from the toy that broke?

Developing Activities

Obviously, you will need to be in or near the church or a home kitchen for this activity.

Making Nutty Butter Cookies (40 minutes)

You will need: 1 cup butter or margarine, softened (250 ml)
2 cups flour (500 ml)
1/2 cup sugar (125 ml)
1 cup finely chopped walnuts (250 ml)
raspberry jam (optional)
baking sheets
rolling pin
small glass or cookie cutter
knife or spatula

Directions: Heat oven to 350 degrees. Mix thoroughly all ingredients. Roll dough 1/4 inch (1.6 cm) thick. Using a glass or cookie cutter, cut out cookies. Place on ungreased baking sheet. Bake 10-12 minutes. If desired, put baked cookies together in "sandwiches" with raspberry jam. This recipe makes seven to eight dozen cookies.

Making the cookies is an activity to help the children begin to think about ways in which they could make or gain some money. As you make the cookies and as you talk about determining costs, the children will get ideas as to labor involved and also the kinds of questions that need to be asked and answered when offering goods or services for sale. It is not intended necessarily that the children be encouraged to bake cookies to sell but rather to have an experience by which to learn what is involved in their cost.

While the cookies are cooling, talk about ways in which children can make money. Of course, one way would be to have a bake sale or a cookie sale. If you decide to do this, check with parents about the use of kitchen equipment.

On a large sheet of newsprint have the children list the ingredients used in making the nutty butter cookies and, beside each item, its approximate cost. (On some items, it will be necessary for leaders to help figure the cost.) Remember to add in some costs for using the oven. What about the value of the work involved? Add the total cost.

Then count the number of cookies that your recipe produced.

Ask the children: If you want to make money on a project like this, how much will you charge per cookie? How much would a potential customer be willing to pay to have a cookie? Is it better to sell cookies individually or by the half or full dozen?

Discuss ways to make the cookies more attractive to the customer. Would you advertise? Would you emphasize that they are "homemade"? What about the packaging? Would it be worth the cost to make the packaging more attractive? Would you list the ingredients so that customers will know you used fresh, wholesome materials in your product? Where would you be selling your cookies?

After discussing how one might sell cookies, let the children enjoy eating them. Talk about the pleasure of eating the cookies after all the hard work and preparation. While you are still enjoying the cookies, help the children to think of other ways in which they could earn extra money. Ask questions like: What are your interests? What do you do best? What would take minimal expenses, resources, and time? Would a neighborhood survey to determine the needs in the community be helpful? Are there things you could do, working in pairs or as a team?

Some possible ideas are: a bike wash, dog wash, craft sale, pet sitting, boot or shoe shines, puppet or magic shows to entertain younger children, garage sale, yard work, housecleaning, picking up mail and newspapers for vacationing or elderly neighbors, plant sitting. The possibilities are endless. List all of their ideas on newsprint as they make their suggestions.

Closing Activities (about 5-10 minutes)

Sitting on the floor in a circle, read the passage from 1 Timothy 6:6-10. Discuss the differences involved in having money and using it wisely and loving money.

Sing the new words to "Row, Row, Row Your Boat":

Make, make, make your dough,
Help to pull a weed.
Take a doggie for a walk,
You can fill a need.

Make up new verses and sing them using different jobs children can do to make money.

Offer a closing prayer asking for help in our search for ways to earn money. Express thanksgiving for our God-given abilities, skills, and interests that will help us to earn money.

Bible Used in This Session: 1 Timothy 6:6-10

Sharing Money

Purposes

- To help children to grow in understanding and appreciating the importance of sharing what we have.
- To help children begin to explore ways to share.

Background for Leader(s)

"Sharing" is a term most children hear and learn about at an early age. Most often, for a child with a sibling, the lesson is painful. The child learns to share toys, to share space, and to share the attention of parents and relatives. "So when and how does sharing become a joyful experience?" one might ask.

In Matthew 6:1-4, Jesus teaches us that giving to a person in need or sharing what we have is a private matter. We are not to show others how good we are by what we give or share. When a child shares a toy with another, he or she may do it in the presence of an adult who then praises the child for his or her generosity. But what if the child shares willingly, without adults looking on? What does the child get out of it? When does sharing become an act of joy?

The answer is quite simple. The joy in sharing comes from the feeling of satisfaction it brings to the one who shares.

Acts 2:43-47 gives another advantage in sharing—it causes a wonderful chain reaction: "All the believers continued together in close fellowship and shared their belongings with one another. They would sell their property and possessions, and distribute the money among all, according to what each one needed" (Acts 2:44-45, TEV). And what did they get in return? ". . . they had their meals together in their homes, eating with glad and humble hearts, praising God, and enjoying the good will of all the people" (Acts 2:46b-47a).

The story of "Billy the Bandage Bandit" will help the children to begin to see what happens when people share. You will need to purchase some inexpensive flexible fabric bandages for the sharing time at the conclusion of this session.

Beginning Activities (10 minutes)

Tell a Story About Sharing

Let the children know that they are going to hear a story. Have them get comfortable, either on the floor or in chairs.

You may either read or tell the following story. Telling it might be more effective if you have the time to learn it well. If you read the story, keep as much eye contact with the children as possible and read with much expression. Children do enjoy having stories read to them. Have some fun with the story!

Billy the Bandage Bandit

by Christopher K. Eng

There once lived a boy named Billy in the city of Johnson City Junction. Billy was about nine years old. He loved soft, tacky, sticky, flexible bandages. He liked to peel open the paper wrapper which kept the brand-new, soft, tacky, sticky, flexible bandages from getting dirty. He enjoyed pulling apart the soft, tacky, sticky, flexible bandages so that the sticky side could be stuck to his arm or leg. "Soft, tacky, sticky, flexible bandages are neat," said Billy. That's because they were waterproof and didn't come off when he took a bath. And they weren't only for cuts and bruises. Billy also stuck them to tree trunks, dogs' ears, and even the walls of his bedroom.

One day, Billy went into a video arcade. The noises of the games went beep-beep, tat-tat, boong-boong, ring-ring, and zap-zap. He began to play with a one-armed bandit. Like some adults who gamble on these machines, Billy hoped that he would strike it rich. But as Billy was playing the game he decided that these video games weren't fun anymore. And as he played, a thought came to him. What if he were to become a bandit himself? What if he held up his friends and robbed them, not of their money, but of their soft, tacky, sticky, flexible bandages? After all, he did need more soft, tacky, sticky flexible bandages to stick on his bicycle and to the wheels of his father's car and on the bottom side of his mother's shoes.

So he went home and worked out a brilliant plan. All he needed was his toy gun, which looked real. So Billy went to his friends and said, "This is a stick-up! Give me all of your soft, tacky, sticky, flexible bandages!" And it worked! But it worked only because Billy's friends thought he was just playing a game. So his friends went along with him and turned over all of their soft, tacky, sticky, flexible bandages to Billy. It wasn't long before Billy went up to strangers and did the same thing. And they gave him all of their soft, tacky, sticky, flexible bandages. Soon, Billy owned all of the soft, tacky, sticky, flexible bandages in town.

Naturally, Billy made sure no one knew the location of his hiding place. He had a huge glass jar in his backyard. At a glance, he could tell if any of his stolen soft, tacky, sticky, flexible bandages were missing. There were soft, tacky, sticky, flexible bandages of all the colors of the rainbow. And there were even Superperson and Dickey Dog soft, tacky, sticky, flexible bandages. Billy's eyes lit up every time he opened the jar to grab a handful to stick on anything and everything.

A strange thing happened in town. Scraped knees and bruised elbows and cut fingers went without the protection of soft, tacky, sticky, flexible bandages. Billy just laughed when he thought of all the people who needed soft, tacky, sticky, flexible bandages but had none. But it wasn't funny to all those people!

One day Billy decided to ride his bike down a steep hill. He didn't see the rocks on the path and swerved too late. There was a twisting of metal, a grinding of teeth, and the scraping of skin as Billy found himself flat on his back. What a sight he was! "Ouch!" he cried. He hurt all over! But he knew he could go home to his secret hiding place and put some soft, tacky, sticky, flexible bandages on his wounds.

What a surprise awaited Billy! One night, Billy had been careless. He had forgotten to close the cover of the soft, tacky, sticky, flexible bandage jar tightly. And it had come loose. Before long, dozens of roaches had begun their invasion of Billy's soft, tacky, sticky, flexible bandage jar. By morning, the roaches had eaten the sticky sides of every soft, tacky, sticky, flexible bandage that Billy had stolen. The soft, tacky, sticky, flexible bandages were now just soft and flexible bandages. He tried to use the soft and flexible bandages, but they wouldn't stick to anything! So Billy began to cry. He felt sorry for himself. Then he began to picture in his mind all of his friends who had stubbed their toes or scraped their elbows. They didn't have any soft, tacky, sticky flexible bandages. They must have cried too!

Billy thought to himself. "What a terrible thing I have done. I will go back to everyone I stole soft, tacky, sticky, flexible bandages from and I will tell all of them how sorry I am. And I'll promise to repay them with twice as many soft, tacky, sticky, flexible bandages." So he went into his room and broke open his piggy bank that had nine years of pennies and nickels and dimes and quarters saved up in it. He asked his sister to drive him to the next town to buy enough soft, tacky, sticky, flexible bandages to repay everyone.

The following day, Billy went from house to house searching for those from whom he had stolen. But when people saw him coming, they cried, "Oh, no! Here comes Billy the soft, tacky, sticky, flexible bandage bandit!" And they began to run away. But Billy caught up with them and gave them back twice as many soft, tacky, sticky, flexible bandages as he had taken from them.

After Billy had repaid everyone, an amazing thing hap-

pened. Everyone began to carry around soft, tacky, sticky, flexible bandages just in case a friend or stranger scraped an arm or cut a finger and needed a soft, tacky, sticky, flexible bandage. And the town was renamed. They decided to call it Flexible Sticky Junction. And somehow, that name still sticks to this day.

When you finish reading or telling the story, ask the following questions of the children. Listen carefully to their answers and encourage the expression of their ideas and feelings about the story. There are no right or wrong answers to these questions. You are interested in knowing how the children understood the story and where they are in their understanding of sharing.

Things to Think About:
1. Why do you think Billy took all the soft, tacky, sticky, flexible bandages from his friends and all the other people?
2. What happened when Billy, at the end of the story, got hurt and needed a soft, tacky, sticky, flexible bandage? What are some of the things he might have been thinking?
3. What do you think this experience taught Billy about the importance of sharing?
4. What wonderful thing happened when Billy repaid everyone?

Making Gift Envelopes (30 minutes)

In this activity the children will be making gift envelopes which they will fill to be given to children in the hospital or in a children's center.

You will need: 7 letter envelopes, legal size, per child
hole puncher
crayons or markers
construction paper
scissors
colorful thick yarn

Give each child 7 envelopes to decorate with colorful drawings or designs. Also, give each one some construction paper with which to make a gift tag. Have the children put their names on their gift tags.

As the children work on this project, ask them to think about things they spend their money on during a typical week. List the items they name on newsprint or a chalkboard. You might expect the list to include candy, gum, baseball cards, video games, batteries, model cars, books, magazines, etc. List whatever the children tell you. Encourage the children to think about sharing some of these things with someone else in the coming weeks. For example, when they purchase a pack of gum, suggest that they think about putting that pack of gum into one of the envelopes. Or if they have enough money, they may want to buy an extra pack to be placed in the envelope. If they spend a quarter playing a video game, they can place an extra quarter in an envelope with a note saying, "You can use this to play video games." You may want to have the children

91

help each other think of possible substitutes for some items which obviously cannot be packaged or placed in one of the envelopes.

After the envelopes have been decorated, use the hole puncher to punch two holes on the flap part of the envelope, approximately 1½ inches (3.8 cm) from the sides. (See diagram A) Thread the yarn through all seven envelopes,

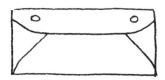

[Diagram A]

[Diagram B]

allowing extra length for the filled envelopes to expand. Tie each length of yarn in a bow, remembering to include the gift tag on one side (see diagram B).

When the envelopes are filled, have the children bring them back to the group. Allow a few weeks for the children to do this. Then plan a trip to a hospital children's ward or a children's center to distribute and share the gifts.

Assignment

Before the children leave, ask them to collect and bring in manufacturers' cents-off coupons for the next session. They will find these in newspapers, magazines, and other sources. They will not need to cut them out individually; the group will have time to do that in Session 3.

Closing Activities (10 minutes)

Form a circle. Learn a new verse to the song you have been singing. (Sing to the tune of "Row, Row, Row Your Boat")

> Share, share, share my dough!
> God will help me see—
> All the love that goes around
> Will soon come back to me.

Give each child a soft, tacky, sticky, flexible bandage. Recall the story of Billy. Remind the children that sharing often causes a happy chain reaction. Encourage each child to help someone this week who is hurting in some way.

Offer a closing prayer.

Bible Used in This Session: Matthew 6:1-4; Acts 2:43-47

Session 3

Saving Money

Purpose

- To help children learn to be good stewards of their money.

Background for Leader(s)

At one time or another we have all heard the saying from Benjamin Franklin's *Poor Richard's Almanack*, "A penny saved is a penny earned." For generations mothers have quoted Ben Franklin as their children ran off to candy stores, movie theaters, and soda shops. As children, some of us have dutifully placed a nickel or dime or quarter every week into a savings account that our parents told us was for our college educations.

Many children are taught the value of saving money, of putting aside some money for "a rainy day," for an emergency, for braces, or for college. Today many children are also being taught another side of saving, that is, how to be good stewards or caretakers of the money they earn or receive.

Stewardship is a term with which most adults have some trouble. We often associate it with giving money to the church. But stewardship means much more than that. It means caring for our resources, managing them well, and using them wisely.

Study Matthew 25:14-30. In this parable of the three servants, Jesus told of a man who left money in the care of his servants while he was away on an extended trip. Two used the money to earn more money, while the third kept his share buried. The first two servants received praise for their good stewardship with the master saying, "Well done, you good and faithful servant!" (v. 21, TEV). The man admonished the third saying, "Well, then, you should have deposited my money in the bank, and I would have received it all back with interest when I returned."

Although children are not in the position of investing much money to make more, they can learn a valuable lesson here. Many may indeed have savings accounts that bear interest, and they can learn to manage wisely the money entrusted to them. In this session, we will look at and think about ways in which children can be good stewards.

Beginning Activities

Play a Guessing Game (15-20 minutes)

As the children arrive, give each one paper and a pencil.

Ask each child to think about the saying: "A penny saved is a penny earned." When all have arrived and had a chance to write down their thoughts, talk with the group about what the saying might mean.

Next, ask each child to write on the other side of the paper one thing he or she can do to save money. The list may include turning off lights when they are not needed, packing a lunch for school instead of buying lunch, taking shorter showers, riding the bike instead of asking Mom to drive, etc. You may need to take a few minutes to discuss openly ways to save money. Children may need help in understanding and thinking of some ways. Then have them write down what each one can do personally.

After everyone has made his or her statement, have the children fold the papers and pass them to the left. Each one then takes a turn to act out what is written on the sheet of paper as the others try to guess what is being acted out. If the children are shy, ask them to do this in pairs or groups, helping each other and sharing ideas.

Developing Activity

Couponing (20-30 minutes)

One way in which many families today save money is to collect manufacturers' cents-off coupons. For this activity you will need to collect ahead of time coupons from newspapers, magazines, and other sources in order to have enough for all the children. At the conclusion of Session 2, the children were asked to collect coupons during the week and bring them for today's session. Be sure to thank those who brought some in.

You will need scissors, paper, and pencils.

Give each person a stack of coupons to cut out. After all the coupons have been cut out, place them face down in the center of the floor.

Give each child paper and pencil. Have each one make a list of ten items his or her family usually needs. Ask the children to limit these items to what they can purchase at a supermarket or grocery store. Examples might be: bread, eggs, toothpaste, toilet paper, trash bags, pet food, cheese, soup, etc.

After they have made their lists, have each person, one at a time in turns, pick up one coupon and try to match it to his or her list. If the coupon doesn't match, set it aside for later. When all the coupons have been taken from the center of the floor, let the children move around and trade coupons with each other. Ask them to try to match every item on their list—or as many as they are able to match. When the matching has been completed (there will be some items not matched), have the children total the savings they will get by using the coupons on their family's next trip to the grocery store.

Encourage the children to think about having coupon exchanges in their church or school to help families with their grocery bills. Talk about ways that couponing can make you a better steward. Also, talk about what could be done with the money saved.

Closing Activities (15 minutes)

Read a story about Benjamin Franklin. You can find excellent children's stories at the public library. A good one to consider is *The Value of Saving: The Story of Benjamin Franklin*, by Spencer Johnson, M.D., (San Diego: Value Communications, Inc., 1978). If you are unable to find a children's book about Benjamin Franklin, do some research and tell a brief story about Franklin to the children.

Form a circle and sing a new verse to "Row, Row, Row Your Boat":

Save, save, save your dough!
You will surely see,
Being stewards is the way
To help your family.

Give a penny to one child. Have the child pass the penny to the person on his or her right and say, "A penny saved is a penny earned." The person who is given the penny will reply "Well done, you good and faithful servant!" (Matthew 25:21), then he or she turns to the next person and passes the penny repeating, "A penny saved is a penny earned." The penny goes all the way around the circle. You may want to start the process or do a practice run with one or two, so everyone will know what to do and feel comfortable. After the circle has been completed, offer a prayer asking God to help us to be good stewards.

Bible Used in This Session: Matthew 25:14-30

Session 4

Spending Money

Purpose

- To help children learn more about what it means to spend money wisely.

Background for Leader(s)

We live in a consumer society. Children learn at a very early age to be consumers. They watch commercials on television aimed at arousing their interest in a particular product, urging them to want and to buy. Their peers encourage them to keep up with the latest fads, the latest clothes, the latest toys. Many adults, by their example, show children that being the ultimate consumer is the "modern way." Being the first on the block to own a new gadget, having the biggest house, owning the most expensive furniture, buying the biggest or sportiest car, wearing the newest designer fashions—all of these become goals that even children begin to accept and work toward. Consumerism is teaching children that to *have* is not enough. To *have more* than others or the *best* is the game most of us are caught in today.

When we study the Bible, we learn about a lifestyle different from our typical lifestyle today. In Hebrews 13:5 we read, "Keep your lives free from the love of money, and be satisfied with what you have. For God has said, 'I will never leave you; I will never abandon you.' " This kind of lifestyle would require Christians to spend money wisely rather than wastefully. It would require being satisfied with less.

Because today's children are consumers, this session will help them to begin exploring the lifestyle being talked about in Hebrews. We will explore and look at some ways this kind of lifestyle might be adapted as their own.

Beginning Activities

Commercial Slogans (20-30 minutes)

Sometime before this session, you will need to make a tape recording (voice only) of television commercials. Try to record between five and ten commercials on the tape, or more if you feel you have time. Get a variety of commercials. If possible, include some of the commercials for candy, toys, games, or sugar-filled breakfast cereals. These are usually aimed at children and can be found on channels

providing children's entertainment, especially Saturday morning cartoons.

As you begin this activity, post a large sheet of paper with the words "TV Commercials" printed across the top. Or you may want to use a large chalkboard, if you have one. Ask the children to list slogans used on television ads. Have them list as many as they can. Some examples are "Coke is it!" "Aren't you hungry for Burger King now?" "Oh what a feeling! Toyota!" "Sorry, Atari!" "Safeguard is the smallest soap in the house!" etc. You will find that children can remember a great number of commercials, and in great detail too.

After the slogans are listed, ask the children to talk about why manufacturers use them. Listen to the children and encourage free expression of their ideas. Then ask the children to close their eyes while you play the tape. Ask them to picture as nearly as they can the scene that goes with each commercial message. After each commercial, stop the tape and ask the children as best they can to describe the scene as it is played on television. Ask the following questions as you discuss what they remember:

1. What is the product? What does it do?
2. Why should I buy it?
3. If it's food, is it healthy?
4. Is it safe? Will it hurt someone?
5. Will I be able to use it a long time?
6. Will I use it often?
7. Will it be as much fun if I use it in my home? Is the commercial misleading in any way? in what way or ways?

When all the commercials have been played and you have discussed each of them, encourage the children to think again about what it means to be a good steward. In what ways can we be good stewards when we are shopping for things we need? What are some ways we teach others to be responsible consumers? Ask the children if they have any tips that they think might help adults spend money more wisely.

Developing Activity

Making Lists of Our Wants and Needs
(30 minutes)

As we continue to think about ways that we spend money and how we might do it more wisely, the next activity is

designed to help children focus on the difference between wants and needs. It will also help children to begin to learn ways of finding the best buy when they have focused on something they plan to purchase.

For this activity you will need:

- paper
- pencils
- a variety of catalogues from sources such as Sears, Penney, Ward, Spiegel, local discount houses, and mail order firms

Each child needs to have paper and pencil. Ask each to make a list of things he or she would like to have. When everyone has completed his or her list, give everyone another sheet of paper. Ask the children to fold the paper in half lengthwise. On one side they will print *Things I Want*; on the other side, *Things I Need*. The next step is to transfer all items on their first lists to the appropriate column on their second sheets of paper. They may wish to work in pairs and discuss their lists with a friend.

Children may need some help with this activity, whether they do it alone or with a friend. The questions below may help them to decide in which column to place items from their first lists. You might want to place the questions on newsprint so that all the children can see them and use them as guidelines.

Things to think about:

- Do I *really need* this item?
- Can I get along without this item for now?
- Is this important to my health or feelings?

After the list has been completed, ask each child to pick out one or two items in their *Things I Need* column, and look them up in the catalogues provided. Remind the children to comparison shop. Look for the same kinds of items in more than one place. Some things to look at for likenesses and differences would be styles, prices, and quality. Ask the children to apply the same set of questions to this task that they used when they were talking about television commercials. The children may want to work in pairs in order to share opinions. Be sure to leave enough time to share or talk about the results of their work.

Closing Activities (10 minutes)

Form a circle. Review with the children all the verses to the song they have learned to the tune of "Row, Row, Row Your Boat." Include this last verse:

Spend, spend, spend your dough!
Spend it carefully.
Learn to use it wisely,
And not too wastefully.

Ask the children to think of something they once purchased and, as soon as they bought it, they regretted having done so. Ask them if they can share the experience with the entire group. Some children may not want to talk about it. Remember to be sensitive to their need for privacy. Some questions you might ask as children share are: How would you do things differently now? What advice would you give to a younger child after your experience?

Ask the children to think about what they have learned in this unit about gaining, sharing, and saving. For those who are willing to do so, ask them to state one thing they have learned.

Offer a prayer of thanks for all the resources God has provided for us. Ask God to help each one of us learn to be good stewards of God's gifts to us.

Bible Used in This Session: Hebrews 13:5

UNIT 7

The Chapel Car Ministry

by Eula Fresch

Unit Introduction

The story of the chapel cars is a fascinating and unique part of the history of American frontier missionary work. The chapel cars were railroad cars built to serve as churches and as living quarters for missionaries establishing new churches in new and remote or isolated towns in the West at the turn of the century. The stories, information, and activities suggested in this unit are designed to help the children visualize, imagine, and experience what the lives and work of the chapel car missionaries might have been like. Choices of projects are presented so that the children can become involved according to their interests and abilities. This is a unit in which the children can have fun learning about and experiencing an important period in mission and ministry.

The focus of this unit is on becoming aware of how new churches were established in the West at the turn of the century. The purpose is to discover the fascinating story of education and evangelism provided by chapel cars and other methods of establishing churches. This unit concentrates on the years between 1890 and 1920 when the chapel cars were at the height of their ministry. The Scripture used is found in Matthew 28:19-20 and 1 John 4:7-12.

Materials to Have Ready

Following are materials you will need for this unit. Some of the supplies may not be needed, depending on which group projects the children choose.

- masking tape
- 4 large appliance or refrigerator boxes

- paint, brushes, jars
- markers
- colored cellophane
- large wall map of the United States
- writing paper and pencils
- construction paper
- scissors
- glue
- fine-point permanent ink markers
- U Film or blank clear filmstrip or slides
  (These can be ordered from Hudson Photographic Industries, Inc., Irvington-on-Hudson, New York, 10533.)
- shoe boxes and other boxes of varied sizes
- poster paper
- paper fasteners
- cardboard
- record player
- Good News Bibles (TEV)

Resources for This Unit

In addition to resources just listed, there are others you will need to get from your local library to make the unit interesting to the children and to provide books and pictures to help the children in their projects. If the ones listed below are not available at your library, your librarian can suggest substitutes. If you visit a local railroad station, you may be able to get free paper engineer hats and other materials. You could also write to major railroad companies for free materials and information about railroad history. The Northern Pacific Railroad, which transported many of the chapel cars, merged with the Burlington Railroad and Great Northern Railroad and is now called the Burlington Northern Railroad Company. It is located at 176 East 5th Street, St. Paul, MN 55101, or 999 3rd Ave., Seattle, WA 98104-4097. The phone numbers are (612) 298-2121 and (206) 467-3838.

The following books give information and pictures about life at the turn of the century:

Cook, Ann, *What Was It Like? When Your Grandparents Were Your Age.* New York: Pantheon Books, 1976

Dunn, Clarice, ed., *We Were Children Then*, Vol. II, edited by Clarice Dunn, Madison: Stanton & Lee Publishing, Inc., 1982

Gard, Robert, ed., *We Were Children Then.* Madison: Stanton and Lee Publishers, Inc., 1976

Pease, Robert, *When Grandfather Was a Boy.* New York: McGraw-Hill Book Co., 1973

This Fabulous Century, 1900-1910, Vol. I. New York: Time-Life Books, 1969.

This Fabulous Century, 1910-1920, Vol. II. New York: Time-Life Books, 1969.

This Fabulous Century, Vol. 8, Prelude, 1870-1900. New York: Time-Life Books, 1969.

Some children's stories about the early 1900s are:

Brink, Carol R., *Louly.* New York: Macmillan Publishing Co., 1974. (Set in Idaho in 1908.)

Smith, E. Boyd, *The Railroad Book.* Boston: Houghton Mifflin Co., 1983. (Originally published in 1913. This story is about a boy and girl who took a train trip west in 1913. The pictures and story would be a great help for the children's projects.)

Sypher, Lucy J., *The Edge of Nowhere.* New York: Atheneum Publishers, 1972. (Set in North Dakota in 1916.)

From your local library you may also be able to get records of train songs and sounds and books on the history of trains which will have pictures and information about the kind of engines and trains used in the West at the turn of the century.

A book which gives the complete story of each of the seven chapel cars is available for sale ($2.50) at the Norwegian Bay Company Store, American Baptist Assembly, Green Lake, WI 54941. The book is *If That Don't Beat the Devil, the Story of the American Baptist Chapel Cars*, by Jacquie McKeon, 1975. However, enough information is provided in this unit that the purchase of this book is not necessary unless you happen to be particularly interested in it.

Resources Included in This Unit

The resources included with this unit are listed below. The pictures should be displayed where the children can refer to them while working on their projects. The stories and other information could be put on tapes for the children to play as needed while working on their projects.

Stories

"A Church on Rails" (p. 102)
"How Colporter Missionaries Traveled" (p. 103)
"How the Chapel Cars Began" (p. 106)
"If You Were a Chapel Car Missionary (Parts 1 and 2)" (p. 109)
"Description of the Cars" (p. 109)

Illustrated Time Line of How Colporter Missionaries Traveled

Songs
"Get on Board"
"Chapel Car *Evangel*"
"From Ocean unto Ocean"

Pictures

Chapel Car *Evangel*

(Both this song and the next are to be sung to the music of "Lead On O King Eternal")

1. Roll on, thou bright *Evangel*!
   Be thine the glorious aim
   To spread abroad the story
   The joyous news proclaim.

Refrain

Across the great wide prairie
By mountains' sloping height
Sing songs of our Lord Jesus,
The darkened world's great light.

2. Roll on, thou bright *Evangel*!
Go like the flying wind
Till all shall know of Jesus,
The Savior of the world.

From Ocean unto Ocean

1. From ocean unto ocean
Our land shall own Thee Lord,
And, filled with true devotion,
Obey Thy sov'reign word:
Our prairies and our mountains,
Forest and fertile field,
Our rivers, lakes, and fountains,
To Thee shall tribute yield.

Get on Board, Children

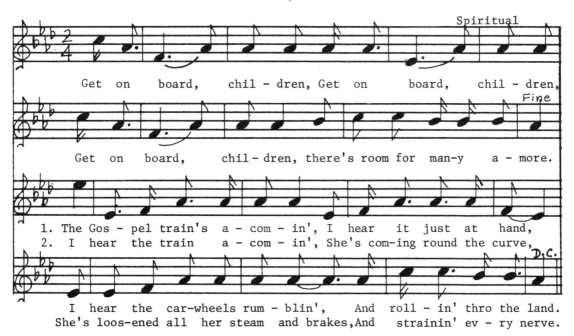

Get on board, chil-dren, Get on board, chil-dren,
Get on board, chil-dren, there's room for man-y a-more.

1. The Gos-pel train's a-com-in', I hear it just at hand,
2. I hear the train a-com-in', She's com-ing round the curve,

I hear the car-wheels rum-blin', And roll-in' thro the land.
She's loos-ened all her steam and brakes, And strainin' ev-ry nerve.

Session 1

A Church on Rails

Purpose

- To introduce the children to the use of chapel cars by early missionaries.
- To introduce the children to some of the history of colporter missionary work.

Background for Leader(s)

Through a "might have been" story the children are introduced to the chapel car ministry. Interest in this subject is stimulated not only by the story but by the beginning conversations the children have about travel and train hobbies. The songs and group projects further encourage enthusiasm about the chapel cars.

It is important for you to be enthusiastic about the subject in order to set the tone for the sessions. Then the children will catch the excitement of this fascinating period in the history of missionary work. It is also important to approach the sessions in a relaxed manner, allowing plenty of time for discussion, sharing of interests and ideas, and the choosing of group projects. A number of projects are suggested so that the children can have a variety of choices and so that they may be stimulated to think of their own projects.

Use the list of questions the children give you in this session to help you plan for the next three sessions. This will help you to respond to the children's interests and help you give them the opportunity to find the answers to them.

The Scripture in this session, 1 John 4:7-12, is used to help the children understand the basic message that the colporter missionaries brought to the isolated areas that they visited. A definition of colporter is included in "How Colporter Missionaries Traveled" at the end of this session.

Gather the supplies listed in the unit introduction and place them in the room. Place any books and pictures you have collected about the period of 1890-1920 around the room.

Using masking tape, mark off a rectangular area on the floor measuring 10 by 40 feet (approximately 3 by 12 meters) to represent the space of the chapel section of the train car. If your room is not that long, just tape two strips of tape 10 feet (3 meters) apart on the floor along the entire length of your room. Or perhaps you could find another area in a larger room for this purpose. Place chairs arranged like the pews in the car *Evangel*. Sitting in an area the size of the chapel will help the children experience what it was like for these early people. To make the taped area seem more like a train car, close in the area with opened-out refrigerator or other large appliance boxes. Cut train windows in the sides and attach colored cellophane to look like stained glass windows across the top third. In large letters print "Chapel Car *Evangel*" on the sides. At the bottom of the sides next to the floor draw wheels.

Print the words to the song "Get on Board" on large newsprint and tape the newsprint on the wall. Plan how you will teach the song.

Beginning Activities

Share Travel Experiences and Hobbies
(10 minutes)

Have a record of train sounds or train songs playing as the children enter. Ask them to join you inside the taped area which represents the chapel car. Invite them to talk about the different ways they like to travel. Ask if any have ridden on trains. Let them tell about the train and where it traveled. Invite those who have trains as a hobby to tell about them.

Read "A Church on Rails" (10 minutes)

Tell the children you are going to read a story about a very unusual train car. (The story is located at the end of this session.) The car is the width of the pretend train car in which they are seated. The story takes place almost one hundred years ago.

After reading the story, tell the children that the chapel car was one way new churches were established in the West from 1890 through the early 1900s. Show pictures of the cars and the interior of the cars. Tell them there were seven chapel cars. *Evangel* was the first, and the Rev. Boston Smith was the first chapel car missionary.

You might ask any or all of the following questions: How would you have felt about the chapel car if you had lived then? How do you think the coming of the car changed a town and its people? What do you think it would have been like to live back in that time? What things would people not have had that they have now? What things could they not do that they do now? Show pictures from the books you collected about the period of time from 1890 to 1920.

Developing Activities

Sing "Get on Board" (5 minutes)

Call the children's attention to the song "Get on Board," which you have posted on the wall. Tell them this was the chapel car song which was sung to the tune of an old spiritual. Sing or play the song for them. Then ask them to sing it with you. Explain that the word "gospel" was used by the missionaries to mean the story of Jesus as found in the four Gospels, which are the first four books of the New Testament—Matthew, Mark, Luke, and John.

If you have time, you might want to sing other railroad songs you or the children may suggest. "I've Been Working on the Railroad" is a good one. If you found a record of railroad songs, you may wish to sing along with one of those songs.

List Questions to Answer (5 minutes)

Ask the children to think of things they would like to find out about the chapel cars, their missionaries, and the establishment of new churches in new western towns. As they state what they want to know, write what they say on a large piece of newsprint. Write it in the form of questions. Tell the children that during these sessions they will have opportunities to discover the answers to their questions.

Group Projects (20 minutes)

Tell the children that they can choose group projects to work on during these four sessions. The number of projects chosen and the number of children in each group will depend on the size of your class and the interests of the children. Tell them about each project and briefly give directions about how it can be done. You will need to decide prior to the session how many and which projects you can offer to the children. Your decision will depend upon your own interests and your ability to get supplies, equipment, and resource persons.

Allow time for the children to think about the projects, discuss them, and see who is interested in which. It would be helpful if you would list the projects on newsprint. Then the children can sign their names by the project they wish to do. Three or four children on one project make up a workable group, although the play and the train layout could use five or six in the group.

Once the groups and projects are decided upon, each group may go ahead and begin its work, using the supplies you have collected. Groups may need help in planning their work and in deciding what other supplies they need and how they will get those supplies.

Following are the projects from which the children may choose:

1. *Build a model train layout for a steam engine and train typical of the early 1900s with a western town and scenery.* Tape the words "*Evangel*" and "*Chapel Car*" on a model train car, or the children could make the car out of boxes. Use shoe boxes and other boxes to build the depot, general store, hotel, etc. to scale. Paper, pieces of wood, and other objects brought from home (such as small toy farm animals and dolls) can be used to complete the scenery and town.

If no one in the class has model trains as a hobby, you might invite a person who does have that hobby to visit the class and help the children set up a layout. Then the children could build the town and countryside to scale.

2. *Make a chapel car out of a long narrow box.* Cut circles of cardboard and attach them to the box with paper fasteners for wheels. Leave the top open and divide up the inside as indicated in the description of *Evangel*. Furnish it like *Evangel*, using clay, tiny boxes, folded paper or cardboard, doll house dishes and furniture, or whatever the children imagine they can use. Colored cellophane can be put across the tops of the windows to look like stained glass.

3. *Make a filmstrip or slide show about the chapel car and show it to the rest of your group.* (You can order blank filmstrip or slides from the U-Film address given in the unit introduction.)

First the children need to write their script telling about the chapel car and the work of the missionaries. Then they decide what pictures they will draw to go with each part of the script. The pictures need to be simple and without much detail. Next cut a strip of heavy paper the width and length of the filmstrip. Draw lines to separate the strip into frames. (You could use an old filmstrip to get the frame size.) Draw the pictures you have planned on the practice strip of paper in the order they need to be to go with the script. Then, using permanent-ink fine-point markers, draw or copy the pictures on the blank filmstrip. Emphasize with the children that the script needs to have one or two sentences to go with each picture and that the pictures must be simple and without detail. When they are ready to show the filmstrip, they can either read the script as each frame is advanced or put the script on a cassette tape.

4. *Write and act out a play.* The children could take one of the stories in these sessions and rewrite it as a play, or they can make up their own play. If they wish to use costumes, they can bring old clothes from their homes.

5. *Make a large map of the United States with train tracks going to the different states where each of the chapel cars went.* (The states that each car visited are listed on page 105.) First the children draw an outline map of the United States showing each state. For the map legend use seven different colors to represent the seven different cars. Paint each state the color corresponding to the car that went there. Use toothpicks to make train tracks winding through each of these states.

6. *Do creative writing related to the chapel cars.* Some children may want to write poems or songs. Some may compose letters pretending they are chapel car missionaries writing about their adventures to family and friends back home.

7. *Make an illustrated time line showing the different ways the colporter missionaries traveled*. Refer to the time line included with the story about colporter missionaries at the end of this session.

8. *Make posters announcing the arrival of a chapel car in a town*. On it can be a picture of the car, information about church services to be held, etc.

Closing Activities (5 minutes)

Invite the children to join you in the "car." Ask in what ways they think the missionaries may have traveled to places that needed churches before the chapel cars came. Read "How Colporter Missionaries Traveled" to the children. Show the illustrated time line.

Closing Worship (5 minutes)

Tell the children that the chapel car missionaries brought the good news of God's love to the people they visited. In the Bible there are many verses about God's love for all of us. 1 John 4:7-12 may have been read by these missionaries to the people who came to church in the chapel cars.

Ask for volunteers to read the verses. Then pray together, thanking God for these early missionaries and the many churches they built.

Bible Used in This Session: 1 John 4:7-12

A Church on Rails

It was a summer day in a young town in Minnesota in the year 1891. Lucy was standing on the train depot platform with her father. She looked expectantly down the track.

"When will it be here, Father? We've been waiting a long time. Do you think we missed it?"

"No," said her father. "Only one train comes through this little town each day, and it hasn't come yet. It will be here soon."

Lucy didn't get to come to town very often. Her family lived on a wheat farm many miles away. It took a long time for them to come in their horse-drawn wagon over dirt roads to get supplies. When Lucy came with her father, they always stopped at the station to see the train come through. This was the most exciting part of the trip for Lucy. She loved trains and she knew the names of all the engines and cars and the things that the cars carried.

Lucy looked down the track again. This time she saw a streamer of smoke. "It's coming!" she yelled excitedly. "It's coming!"

She heard a double whistle warning, and then the huge black engine steamed into view. She covered her ears to muffle the sound of the powerful engine. Dust and cinders flew everywhere as the engine pulled past the station.

Lucy named the cars as they passed by—a tender full of coal, hopper cars full of iron ore from Minnesota's mines, covered hopper cars full of wheat and other grains, flat cars with lumber from Minnesota's forests, cattle car, box car, Pullman sleeper? Pullman sleeper? No, it wasn't a Pullman sleeper. This car was different, and why would it be at the end of a freight train? Lucy had never seen a car like this before. She read the words on the side—"Chapel Car *Evangel*." Lucy was puzzled. "Father, look at that car. What is it?"

"I don't know," her father said. Others on the platform began talking about the car too. Then Lucy heard the engine's air brakes go *sssssssssss*.

"Look, the train is stopping," shouted Lucy excitedly.

"I wonder why it's stopping," said her father. This town is so small and new that the train usually throws off the mail as it steams through without stopping.

Lucy and her father went over to where the train had stopped. They saw some railroad men uncouple the new car and sidetrack it. Then the train steamed on toward Duluth.

"Let's get a closer look at that car," said Lucy to her father. As they approached the car along with other curious onlookers, a man came out of the car and introduced himself.

"I'm the Reverend Boston Smith," he said.

"What kind of car is this?" asked Lucy after Mr. Smith had met everyone in the group.

"This is a church car," he said. It also has a small apartment for me to live in while I travel. Would you like to come in and see it?"

"We sure would," said Lucy and her father. Lucy went aboard with the others. She had never been in a church. There was no church in this town or anywhere near them. Inside the car she stood looking around in amazement. She saw pews with hymnal racks on the back, a pump organ, a pulpit, and brass chandeliers hanging from the domed ceiling. She saw small stained-glass windows above the regular train windows. Rev. Boston Smith reached into one of the storage boxes under one pew and got out Bibles and tracts. He handed each person a tract telling about the ministry of the chapel car.

"I'm holding a church service every night this week and twice on Sunday," he said. "There will also be church school this Sunday afternoon for all of the children. I'd like you all to come. Please invite your families and friends, too."

Lucy and her father stayed after the others in the group had left. "Can we see the rest of the car?" asked Lucy.

"I'll be glad to show it to you," said Mr. Smith as he led them around a divider into the living quarters.

"This little room serves as my study, dining room, and living room," said the minister. Looking around, Lucy saw a writing desk, bookshelves going all the way up to the ceiling, and a table. In another section she saw an upper and lower berth like those in the Pullman sleeping cars.

Then Mr. Smith led them around a passageway where there was a little kitchen with a small stove, a copper-lined sink connected with a tank overhead. There was a sideboard and a china closet, too. In the back of this area was a small bathroom.

"I've never seen a car like this," said Lucy as they walked back into the chapel portion of the car.

"It's the only one," said Mr. Smith. "It's a church and parsonage on wheels. Many of our new towns out here in the West don't have churches. With this car I can bring a church to them."

"How long will you be sidetracked here?" asked Lucy's father.

"As long as it takes to get a church started," said the minister.

"We are heading over to the drugstore to get ice cream," said Lucy's father. "Would you like to come with us? We'll be glad to show you around our town."

"I'd like to do that," said Mr. Smith. "I need to put some posters in the stores inviting people to come to the church services."

Mr. Smith got the posters and they stepped out of the chapel car and started into town. The town was young, so there were only a few buildings. Lucy and her father helped Mr. Smith put up the posters in the bank, the general store, the hotel, and even the saloon. After putting up a poster in the drugstore, they all sat down and enjoyed their ice cream.

After they had finished, Mr. Smith said, "Thank you for showing me around. Now I need to get a horse and start calling on the people who live around here. I hope to see you at some of the church services in the chapel car."

"We'll try to come," said Lucy's father. "We live some distance from town, you know. Good-bye."

"I can hardly wait to tell Mother and Lewis about the church train car," Lucy said as they left the drugstore. "Can we come back to the services?"

"Maybe we can come Sunday," said her father. "Now let's get started home. We have a long ride."

The trip back home took longer than usual. It began to rain, and the dirt road became muddy. When the wagon wheels got stuck, Lucy and her father had to get out and push the wagon free. When they finally got home, Lucy helped her father unharness the two horses and put them in the barn. Then she raced into the kitchen.

"Mother! Lewis!" she shouted. "The train stopped in town and sidetracked a new car."

"What kind of car is it?" asked Lewis as he hurried into the kitchen. Lewis was Lucy's younger brother. He had only been into town once, and he loved to hear Lucy tell about her adventures there. He could hardly wait until he was old enough to go too.

"It's a church car, a chapel car called *Evangel*," said Lucy. "And I got to go inside it."

"Tell us about it," said Mother as she came into the room. And Lucy told them all about the car and about Mr. Smith.

"There are services each night and twice on Sunday," said Lucy. "And there's a special church school for children."

When Father came in, Lewis asked, "Can we go, Father? I've never been to church. I'd like to see what it's like."

"I used to go to church back East before we moved out here," said Mother. "I miss the church."

"Mr. Smith says he is going to help build one here," said Father. "We'll go this Sunday to the church service in the chapel car if it's not raining."

"Oh, thank you, Father," said Lewis and Lucy together as they hugged their father.

Lewis and Lucy could hardly wait until Sunday. Mother was excited, too. She didn't get to see other people very often, because the farms were so far apart and the trip to town was long. She and Lucy began to bake bread and cakes to take with them for lunch on Sunday.

Finally Sunday came. They packed food for the day in the wagon and hitched up the two horses. They started out early, but by the time they got there the service had already started. The organ was playing and people were singing. They slipped quietly into the back of the car and sat down. After more singing, Mr. Smith read from the Bible in the fourth chapter of the book of 1 John. Then he talked to the people about God's love for them. The service ended after they sang a few more hymns.

Lucy and her family went to their wagon to eat lunch and visit with other families. That afternoon the children were invited back to the chapel car for church school. Before they left to return to their farm, Mr. Smith talked to Lucy's father and some other men about starting a church in their town. They agreed to meet next Sunday after the service to begin planning for their town's church.

On the way home Lewis and Lucy talked excitedly about the church school. "There were so many children," said Lucy. "Big children had to hold smaller ones on their laps so that we could all fit into the car."

"We got to listen to music on the gramophone," said Lucy. "We learned a new song. It's called 'Jesus Loves Me.' " Then Lewis and Lucy sang "Jesus Loves Me" as they rode home. They could hardly wait until next Sunday to come back to the church on rails.

How Colporter Missionaries Traveled

The missionaries who served on the chapel cars were called colporters. They were named after the early missionaries who traveled on foot. The word "colporter" comes from the French *colporteur*, which means "neck-peddler." These earliest missionaries walked from place to place telling the people the good news about Jesus and about God's love for everyone. Because they carried Bibles and tracts in bags hung from wooden yokes around their necks and on their shoulders, they were called colporters. They knocked on doors and gave pamphlets or tracts and Bibles to those who would accept them. They preached and they taught. They organized church schools and churches. Later these colporters traveled on horseback.

Still later, the colporters used wagons or buggies with teams of horses to bring the Word of God to people. The colporter's wagon served as his home while he traveled. The wagon had a built-in bed behind the seat. There was a drawer under the bed to hold Bibles and tracts. A canvas covered the bed to keep out road dust and rain. At the back of the wagon the tailgate opened to form a table. There was a metal box for food supplies and an iron cook stove. Two nose bags, sacks of oats, and a watering pail were carried for the horses.

Finally, in 1891, chapel train cars began to be used. Later methods of travel for the missionaries, other than train, were motor boat, automobile, bus, and auto trailer. Whatever method they used to travel, the colporter missionaries all had one goal. They were dedicated to carrying out Christ's words in Matthew 28:19-20.

Here is an illustrated time line showing their different methods of travel and the dates each way of travel began.

(Show the children the illustrated time line.)

During the century of 1840-1940 the colporter missionaries accomplished the following:

Families visited	6,094,150
Conversions	335,989
Baptisms	71,856
Churches organized	4,008
Church schools organized	17,565
Miles traveled by auto, rail, and mule	8,618,687

1840   1891   1940

ON FOOT   ON HORSEBACK   BY CHAPEL CAR   BY WAGON   BY MOTOR BOAT   BY AUTOMOBILE   BY CHAPEL BUS   BY AUTO TRAILER

Session 2

How It All Began

Purpose

- To help the children understand how the chapel cars began.
- To help the children appreciate the work of the chapel car missionaries.

Background for Leader(s)

The story in this session tells about the origin of the idea for chapel cars, how the cars were built, the need for the cars, and the work made possible by the seven cars.

At the close of this session the children will participate in a pretend dedication of *Evangel* to help them gain an appreciation for the work of the missionaries who used these cars. The Scripture used is Matthew 28:19-20, which is Jesus' command to take his message to all people everywhere. Through the use of the Scripture in the dedication service the children can be helped to understand how dedicated the chapel car missionaries were to carrying out this command.

To prepare for this session, put a large map of the United States on the wall. Print the dedication song, "Chapel Car *Evangel*" on large newsprint and post it on the wall. Become familiar with the song and plan how you will teach it. Gather all the materials needed for projects chosen last week.

Beginning Activities (5 minutes)

Invite the children to join you in the "chapel car," (the taped-in area). Sing together, "Get on Board" and "I've Been Working on the Railroad." Introduce the song, "Chapel Car *Evangel*" by saying that this was written especially for the dedication of this first car in 1891. Play or sing the song for them. Then ask them to sing it with you as they read the words of the song printed on newsprint. If you do not play an instrument or sing with comfort, ask someone who does either or both easily to put it on tape for you. Use the tape to help your group learn the song.

Developing Activities

Read "How the Chapel Cars Began"
(10 minutes)

Talk about the story read in Session 1, "A Church on Rails." Ask the children how they think the idea for chapel cars might have begun. Tell them that the story you are going to read to them explains how it actually happened.

(This story is located at the end of this session.)

After reading the story, ask the children how they would have felt about the building and use of the cars if they had been Rev. Boston Smith and each of the other people mentioned in the story.

Show a map of the United States. Ask for volunteers to find the different states where the cars went as you call out the car's name and the states for each car. Talk about how the missionaries were able to visit people and establish churches in isolated areas in these states because they could travel by rail in these chapel cars.

Following is a list of the cars and some of the states they visited:

Evangel: Minnesota, Oklahoma, Wyoming, Kansas, North Dakota, Montana, Missouri, Arkansas

Emmanuel: Colorado, California, Oregon, Washington, Idaho

Glad Tidings: Montana, Arizona, Minnesota

Good Will: Colorado, Idaho, Texas

Messenger of Peace: Washington, Kansas, Missouri, California

Herald of Hope: West Virginia, Ohio, Illinois, Michigan, Iowa

Grace: California, Nevada

Plan for Dedication Service (30 minutes)

Tell the children that at the end of this session they will participate in a pretend dedication service of *Evangel*. Ask for three or four volunteers to plan with you for that service before they start their group projects. After several children volunteer, the rest of the children can go ahead and start their group project work.

Suggest that one of your volunteers pretend to be Dr. Hoyt, the pastor who says the actual words of dedication for *Evangel*. Another volunteer can read Matthew 28:19-20, explaining that the chapel car missionaries were dedicated to doing what these verses said. A third child can lead the group in singing the dedication hymn learned at the beginning of this session. A fourth can introduce each of the other three who have parts in the service. After they decide who is going to do which part of the service, let them work on their parts and practice if they wish. When they feel ready for the dedication, they may join in the work on their group projects.

Group Projects (30 minutes)

Allow plenty of time for the children to work on these projects. Check with each group to see whether they need any information or supplies or any help in doing their projects. Some groups may finish their projects at the end of this session or the next session. If so, they may choose another project or devise one of their own that is not too involved, so that they will have time to complete it before the final session of the unit.

Closing Activity

Pretend Dedication Service of *Evangel* (15 minutes)

Ask the children to join you inside the chapel car (taped-in area). The group who planned this service with you earlier will lead the service. One of the volunteers will introduce Dr. Hoyt. The child pretending to be Dr. Hoyt will say something like, "We dedicate this car to bringing missionaries to new towns where there are no churches." The child can also say something about what the missionaries will do. After this the children who planned to read the Scripture and lead the song will do their parts. One of the leaders could close by leading in prayer, thanking God for the missionaries and their work made possible by the chapel car.

> **Bible Used in This Session**: Matthew 28:19-20

How the Chapel Cars Began

It was the year 1879, and winter was coming. A colporter missionary in a new town in southeastern Minnesota had a big problem. Over sixty people came to his outdoor church and church school meetings. That turnout was wonderful, but soon it would be too cold to continue meeting outdoors under a tent. There were only a few buildings in the little village. None of them was big enough to hold that many people. What was he to do? He walked around the village thinking about the problem. He came to the train station and saw some passenger cars sidetracked. Seeing the cars gave him a great idea. Why not borrow a passenger coach each weekend for his meetings? Quickly he wrote the supervisor of the Northern Pacific Railroad telling about his problem and asking him to lend a passenger coach each weekend to be used as a church. Soon the answer came. It was yes!

So each Saturday a passenger coach was sidetracked in his town for the church school and church meetings. Each Monday, the coach was picked up by the daily express. Because of the railroad's help, the missionary was able to continue his work, and a church was built in that village.

Now at that time Rev. Boston Smith was supervisor of Baptist missionaries in Minnesota. He heard about the missionary's use of a train car for a church. "What a great idea!" he thought. "Why, I can imagine taking a church car from town to town bringing missionaries and a church to lonely places that have never had a church." His dream of a "church on rails" began to grow, but it was to be twelve years before his dream was realized.

Rev. Smith knew that dreams do not come true by themselves. So he talked about his dream with other people. He talked with Dr. Wayland Hoyt, who was the pastor of the First Baptist Church in Minneapolis. Dr. Hoyt's brother, Colgate Hoyt, was an executive of the Northern Pacific Railroad.

One day when Dr. Hoyt and his brother were on a train trip through Minnesota and Wisconsin, Dr. Hoyt looked out the windows as the train rushed along the track past new towns. He saw that most of these new towns did not have a church. He said to his brother, "Why can't a missionary car of some kind be built to go to these lonely towns and give the people a chance to hear about the gospel?"

"I will think about it," said his brother. After Dr. Hoyt went back home, he got a letter from his brother saying he had organized a group of businessmen to arrange for the building of a church car. Dr. Hoyt excitedly called on Rev. Smith and told him of his brother's offer.

"Please draw up a plan for a railroad car in which a missionary can both live and hold services," he told Rev. Smith.

So Rev. Smith worked with an architect on the plan and gave it to the group of businessmen. They had the Barney Smith Car Company in Dayton, Ohio, build the car. From there the car went to Minneapolis and St. Paul, where it was furnished by the women of the Baptist churches there.

The car was named *Evangel* and dedicated in 1891. At this dedication service a hymn was sung which was written especially for the dedication of *Evangel*.

But Rev. Smith still had work to do. He had to persuade the railroad executives to transport the car over their lines. He went to see Mr. Mellon, who was general manager of the Northern Pacific Railroad. Mr. Mellon offered *Evangel* (and future cars) free travel over the Northern Pacific Railroad lines. He gave orders for the car to be coupled to any train the missionary chose. This was a wonderful gift.

On the first trip *Evangel* traveled one thousand miles west of Minneapolis, with Rev. Boston Smith serving as her first missionary. As she rolled through Minnesota, North Dakota, and Montana, she was sidetracked from one to three days at a time.

Evangel's work was so successful that another car was needed. Money was donated for the second car. It was named *Emmanuel* and dedicated in 1893. On the day *Emmanuel* was dedicated, money was donated for a third car. It was named *Glad Tidings* and dedicated in 1894. In 1895 the fourth chapel car, *Good Will*, was dedicated. The fifth,

Messenger of Peace, was dedicated in 1898. *Herald of Hope*, number six, was dedicated in 1900, and the seventh, *Grace*, was dedicated in 1915.

As each new car was added, the missionaries were able to visit more areas of need. The first car began by traveling to people in Minnesota. By the time the seventh was in service, the cars had been over railroad lines going from Minnesota to California, from Texas to West Virginia, including the Colorado mountains and most of the Midwest.

The work of the chapel car missionaries was so successful that by 1905 they had already established a total of 135 churches, 112 meeting houses, and 243 church schools. They had baptized 4,578 people. All this in only fourteen years!

By 1913 the total number of churches established had grown to 180, the number of meeting houses to 149, the number of church schools to 298, and the number of people baptized to 17,194. Imagine how the people and the towns were changed because of the great work made possible by the chapel cars!

Session 3

The Work and Life of Chapel Car Missionaries

Purpose

- To help the children understand and appreciate the work of the chapel car missionaries.
- To help the children imagine what it was like living on the cars.

Background for Leader(s)

As you work through this session and Session 4, be sure that you provide opportunities for the children to find the answers to the questions they listed in Session 1. Continue to work with each of the groups as needed. Groups that finish during this session will need guidance in choosing another project they can complete in Session 4. Print the words to "From Ocean unto Ocean" on newsprint.

During this session the children will have the opportunity to imagine themselves as chapel car missionaries. Through the information given in this session and the skits, they can be helped to feel and experience what it may have been like for these early missionaries. They can have fun spontaneously acting out these skits of situations they might have faced if they themselves were chapel car missionaries at the turn of the century.

Beginning Activities

Sing "I've Been Working on the Railroad," "Get On Board" and "Chapel Car *Evangel*."

Read "If You Were a Chapel Car Missionary," parts 1 and 2, and then discuss both parts.

Encourage the children to talk about what they think it was like living on the chapel cars and doing the work of the missionaries. Tell them this story asks them to pretend they are chapel car missionaries and experience what it was like then. Tape an area 10 by 18 feet (3 by 5.5 meters) on the floor to help them imagine what it was like to live in this space when it was filled with furniture. Share the information in "Description of the Cars." Show the picture of the inside of the car. You might have the children close their eyes as you read the story, if this helps them to pretend and to picture what happened. Read the story or tell it, and then discuss it with the children.

Developing Activities

Do Skits About the Experiences of Chapel Car Missionaries (15 minutes)

After reading the stories and talking about them, ask the children to list some situations chapel car missionaries faced. You might write them on newsprint as the children recall them. Then ask for volunteers to act out these situations spontaneously for the whole group. Give a few minutes for each group to plan how they will act out their situation, and then let them act it out for the whole group. If necessary, you might suggest some of the following:

(a) Your chapel car has just arrived in a farming town. You visit, invite people to come, etc.

(b) Your chapel car has just arrived in a rough mining town where you are not welcome. Act out what happens and how you win the town over.

(c) Act out cooking, eating, and living on the car.

(d) Act out holding a church school in the car.

(e) Temporarily sidetracked in a railroad yard, you visit the railroad men and hold a midnight-shift service.

Work on Group Projects (30 minutes)

Each group formed in Session 1 will continue to work on projects started then. If any group finishes its project, it may choose another to begin, or the children may choose to do individual projects. Projects 6 and 8 suggested in Session 1 would make good individual projects that could be completed during this and the next session.

Closing Activities (10 minutes)

Call the children's attention to the words of the hymn "From Ocean unto Ocean" printed on newsprint. Read it together. Tell them the music of this hymn was used with the song "Chapel Car *Evangel*." Sing the song together.

Close the session by reading from 1 John 4:7-12. Remind the children that these verses are part of the message the missionaries took to the places they visited. Offer a prayer thanking God for people who share the good news of God's love with people everywhere.

Bible Used in This Session: 1 John 4:7-12

If You Were a Chapel Car Missionary

Part 1: Your Work

Pretend you are a colporter missionary on the chapel car *Glad Tidings* in the winter of 1899. You are planning to sidetrack in Frazee, Minnesota, on Wednesday and hold church services that night. So you send ahead your arrival date and the time of the service along with a photograph of your car. When the dispatcher hears this, every ticket agent along the line knows you are coming. As you go through each station, people are waiting to see the chapel car.

You do not wait until you get to Frazee to begin your work. You have been coupled to the end of a passenger train. Every two hours you hold services for the passengers while the train is racing along the tracks.

After all the passengers get off, the train stops at a railroad yard to have the shop make some repairs. You hold a lunchtime service for the railroad workers. While they eat lunch in the car, they listen to gramophone music and to your sermon. Many of these workers are far from home and lonely. Many have never been to church.

Then you go into the yard shop and talk to the workers. You leave tracts and Bibles. They ask you to have a service for them during their midnight break because they are on the night shift. So at midnight you plan and carry out a special service for them.

The next morning you are on your way again. When you arrive at Frazee, the weather is cold and it has been snowing. However, there is a crowd of people waiting to see the car and attend the service. The side track is blocked with slack (a combination of fine coal, slate, and dirt) and snow. You get a scoop shovel and help clear it. Then you help with the uncoupling and sidetracking of your car, and you hold your first church service in Frazee.

You visit with the people in town the next morning. Then you get a horse and go out into the countryside. You go into the fields or barns where men are working and talk to them about coming to your church services. You hand out more Bibles and tracts.

After being in the little town for awhile and organizing a church and a church school, you go out and raise money for the church building. You even do some carpentry work with the workers who are putting up the building. All during this time you continue holding church and church school.

You have been working sixteen or more hours a day during the month you have been in Frazee. Now it is time for you to go on to another town. You arrange for the new church to get a pastor who will live there. Then you couple onto the next train coming through and travel on to the next town in need of a church.

Part 2: Living in the Car

Pretend you are a new missionary living in a chapel car. You are finding that it is a lot more work than you imagined.

You are doing many more things in addition to regular missionary work of teaching, preaching, visiting, handing out Bibles and tracts, building churches, playing the organ, singing, and baptizing people. You and your helper also have to be janitor, cook, and railroad helper.

You help with the coupling and uncoupling of the car and with the sidetracking. You even make simple repairs on the cars.

You often find living in such a small space to be frustrating. Your kitchen is only four feet square. Into that space are fitted a sink, stove, icebox, and china closet. There is hardly room to turn around. If you happen to be cooking or eating when the train suddenly stops or coupling is being done, dishes and food might fly to the floor.

The study also serves as the bedroom. If you are meeting with someone, your helper has to go into the chapel or go outside.

Some people in some of the rougher towns sometimes don't want the car in their town. They are against the work missionaries are trying to do. Once someone painted ''cattle car'' on the chapel car. Another time people threw eggs at it. When these things happen, you pretend to ignore them. You just clean it off and go on with your work, and you make an effort to be friendly and loving to the people who are against what you are doing. Sometimes these people change and become strong workers in the church.

There is not much privacy living in the car. Wherever you go, the car attracts a lot of attention. Crowds of people come to see it. Newspapers write about it. Many times so many people want to come to the services that there isn't enough space for them all in the car.

In spite of these things, you are dedicated to helping people in these isolated areas hear about God's love for them. You are thankful for the chapel car, because it makes your work possible. You are thankful for all of the churches that have been established because of the ministry of the chapel cars.

Description of the Cars

Evangel's total size was 60 by 10 feet (18.3 by 3 meters). The inside was divided into two parts—the living quarters and the chapel. Large storage boxes under the car held coal, ice, and wood. A hot water system heated the car in the winter. It was lighted by acetylene gas.

The chapel could seat 80 to 100 people in hardwood pews on each side of the aisle. For church school 150 children sometimes crowded into the pews. The pews seated three people on the right and two on the left of the aisle. Hymnal racks were attached to the back of each pew. Under the pews were storage boxes for Bibles and tracts. There was a deacon's bench at the front of the chapel, an Estey pump organ, a brass pulpit, and a blackboard. There were brass chandeliers hanging from the ceiling and small stained glass window panes above the windows.

The living quarters took up a space of 10 by 18 feet (3 by 5.5 meters) of the total car. There was a combination dining room and parlor furnished with tables, a rolltop desk, and bookshelves going up to the ceiling. There was a bed-room with an upper and lower berth, a kitchen, a pantry, and a toilet room. The kitchen had a stove, an icebox, and a china closet. There was a copper-lined sink connected with a tank overhead.

Session 4

Sharing Our Work About the Chapel Car Ministry

Purpose

- To give the children the opportunity to share with each other the projects and information they have worked on during these sessions.

Background for Leader(s)

In this session no new information is introduced except for the story of what happened to the cars. Time is spent in this session in finishing group projects and in sharing these projects with the total class. Check to see whether you need to gather some materials and equipment that some groups may need in order to share their projects. For example, the group making a filmstrip or slides will need a projector.

This session can be the most enjoyable one of all these sessions for the children. Allow plenty of time for them to share their projects.

Beginning Activities

"What Happened to the Chapel Cars?" (10 minutes)

Ask the children why they think chapel cars are not used today. What do they think happened to the cars after they were no longer used? Then read the story "What Happened to the Chapel Cars?" Show the picture of Chapel Car *Grace,* which is now located at the American Baptist Assembly, Green Lake, Wisconsin.

Developing Activities

Finish Group Projects (10 minutes)

The children will finish their projects and plan how they will present them to the total class. Those who are ready before others could write newspaper articles about what happened to the cars after they stopped being used.

Sharing Group Projects (35 minutes)

Each group will show their project or projects to the whole group and also share any information they found about the chapel cars and the missionaries that would be interesting to the group.

If the sharing of projects needs more time, you will need to revise either your beginning or closing activities to gain more time.

Singing (5 minutes)

Sing "Get on Board," "Chapel Car *Evangel*" and "From Ocean unto Ocean."

Read Matthew 28:19a and 20a.

Remind the children that the chapel cars made it possible for these early missionaries to "go to all people." Get their ideas about how missionaries today "go to all people," how they travel, what they do, etc. Then ask them to think about ways they can share God's love with other people today. (Some might suggest inviting friends to church, showing love to others by doing kind and helpful things, etc.)

Closing Activities (5 minutes)

Close with a prayer asking God to help us today to share the story of Jesus and God's love with others.

> **Bible Used in This Session:** Matthew 28:19-20

What Happened to the Chapel Cars?

As more and more people began to use atuomobiles, and better roads were built, the need for the chapel cars was not as great. By 1943 chapel cars were no longer used. Where are the cars now?

Some were put inside churches being built. *Evangel* became part of the First Baptist Church of Rawlins, Wyoming, a church that this car helped to establish. *Glad Tidings* became part of the First Baptist Church in Flagstaff, Arizona. *Grace* is at the American Baptist Assembly in Green Lake, Wisconsin, where she is used for chapel services. *Emmanuel* is being restored in Madison, South Dakota, and is in the Prairie Village Museum there. If you go to any of the places where these cars are, be sure to visit them. You'll feel as though you're seeing a friend.

UNIT 8

Saints of God

by Steve Edwards

Unit Introduction

The focus of this unit is on All Saints' Day. This festival, formerly known in Britain as All Hallows' Day, is observed to commemorate all Christian saints and martyrs. The night before the festival is commonly called Halloween (Hallows Eve). It was once believed that on this night witches, devils, goblins, and other fairy-like creatures came out for their annual holiday. The modern practice of dressing in costumes and trick-or-treating, although a delightful custom and a joy for most children, is based on these dreadfully pagan beliefs. We would do well in the church not to make more of Halloween than the simple joy it has become, and to help focus our children's thoughts on the saints for whom the original festival was intended. Perhaps one or more of the sessions in this unit could be used on or around Halloween to make children aware of All Saints' Day, which has been sadly neglected in Protestant churches.

The purpose of this unit is to help children see sainthood as a quality found in devoted followers of Jesus today and throughout history. Although it includes some treatment of historic individuals who are generally recognized as saints, the main emphasis is on the qualities of sainthood in all devoted followers of Christ. After studying this unit the children should be able to:

1. identify at least three characteristics of sainthood
2. name at least two "official" saints and tell something of their lives
3. list three or four specific things they can do to make their own lives saint-like

114

Who Are the Saints of God, Anyway?

Many stories from movies and books portray a saint as either a person who always does the right things—things no one else wants to do, or someone possessing power far beyond what is common in human beings. Most of us would not want to be such a person. The biblical picture, however, is quite different.

The Old Testament refers to persons of unusual holiness and consecration as saints (Psalms 31:23, 106:16, KJV). At the same time, the entire nation of Israel is described as a "congregation of saints" (Psalms 149:1, KJV). Apparently all of the chosen are considered to be saintly.

The same is found in the New Testament. Paul says that Christians are "called to be saints" in Jesus Christ (Romans 1:7). The Christians at Lydda and at Ephesus were called "holy ones" or "saints" (Acts 9:32; Ephesians 1:1). All Christians are the saints of God.

Synonyms for the Old Testament meaning of "saintly," include "caring," "compassionate," "godly," and "holy." In the New Testament the Greek word for "saint," *hagios*, implies a separateness. Saints are separated from sin and thus consecrated to God. Certainly these characteristics are desirable for all Christian people.

"Official" Saints

As early as the second century the church began to recognize certain individuals as persons of exceptional holiness and, as a special honor, gave them the official title of "saint." It is common practice in churches to use this title in reference to many New Testament figures such as St. Paul and St. Peter; and church historians are very familiar with St. Augustine, St. Francis, and St. Catherine of Siena, among others. Countless other people throughout history have exemplified the teachings of Christ in ways that bring honor to God and God's church. The Roman Catholic Church is still giving this honorary title to deserving individuals. Protestants uphold their saints in different ways.

Certainly the lives of these saints of God can be an inspiration to each of us as we struggle with our own calls to holiness. There is no better model after whom to pattern one's own life than Christ himself.

Materials to Have Ready

Session 1:
- large red heart
- large green shamrock
- newsprint
- colored felt-tip markers
- gift wrap

- gold glitter
- aluminum foil

Session 2:
- magazines
- newsprint or posterboard
- Kodak Ektagraphic write-on slides or old filmstrips

Session 3:
- pipe cleaners
- cotton balls
- colored chalk, markers, tempera paints
- colored construction paper
- glue
- aluminum foil

Session 4:
- finger paint (or starch and poster paint)
- glossy paper
- aprons
- newspapers to protect tabletops

Resources for This Unit

Armstrong, Edward A., *Saint Francis: Nature Mystic.* Berkeley: University of California Press, 1973. (For background reading.)

Attwater, Donald, *The Penguin Dictionary of Saints.* New York: Penguin Books, 1984. (A catalogue with brief descriptions of the principal saints in the Roman Catholic Church.)

Bettenson, Henry, ed., *Documents of the Christian Church.* New York: Oxford University Press, 1970. (Contains the Rule of Saint Francis. For background reading.)

Corfe, Tom, *Saint Patrick and Irish Christianity.* New York: Cambridge University Press, 1973. (Children will enjoy the many pictures and drawings which bring Saint Patrick alive.)

Doyle, Eric, *Saint Francis and the Song of Brotherhood.* New York: The Seabury Press, 1980. (For background reading.)

Ebon, Martin, *Saint Nicholas Life and Legend.* New York: Harper & Row Publishers, Inc., 1975. (The illustrated story of how the revered Bishop Nicholas of Myra evolved into jolly old Santa Claus.)

Harbin, Robert, *Origami, The Art of Paperfolding.* New York: Barnes & Noble Books, 1982. (Suggested for use in Session 3.)

Jones, Charles W., *Saint Nicholas of Myra, Bari, and Manhattan.* Chicago: University of Chicago Press, 1978. (For background reading.)

Post, W. Ellwood, *Saints, Signs and Symbols.* Wilton, Conn.: Morehouse-Barlow Co., Inc., 1974. (The children may enjoy seeing the symbols of many of the saints. Suggested in Session 4.)

Session 1

Called to Be Saints

Purpose
- To enable children to explore qualities and characteristics of persons whom the church has named as saints throughout history and to accept the challenge to be saint-like.
- To help children to understand the connection between the origin of Halloween and the celebration of All Saints' Day.

Background for Leader(s)

As stated in the unit introduction, the qualities of sainthood mentioned in the Bible are the ability to be caring, compassionate, godly, holy, and consecrated. These are difficult concepts to teach to children, so this session will attempt to do it only on a limited basis. If the children understand that a saint is one who cares for all people even when threatened with personal injury, and one who forgives those who have inflicted personal injury, then the teaching/learning process has been effective.

This objective will be accomplished by briefly studying the stories of two saints of whom all the children will have heard—Saint Valentine and Saint Patrick. The stories are simple and need no comment here. This session also contains a brief study of 2 Corinthians 5:16-21. The appropriate emphasis is that as saints we need to be helping to turn enemies into friends. Verse 17 gives the promise that change is possible, and verse 18 states the challenge.

Do not take too much time with the opening activities related to Halloween. Remember, the focus is on All Saints' Day. The Halloween activities serve only to catch the attention of the children.

Allow plenty of time for the learning centers. It is important that the children actively respond to the stories and the Scripture in order to make the learning much more effective.

The activities related to the song "I Sing a Song of the Saints of God" and the final sharing are aimed at having the children understand that all Christians are called to be saints, which is one of the major objectives of the session.

In preparation for this session:
- make a large red heart and a large green shamrock.
- make an all saints' shield, or at least begin it, to show the children.

Beginning Activities

Halloween Memories (5 to 10 minutes)

Post four pieces of newsprint on the wall with one of the following headings on each:

—What I like most about Halloween
—This year for Halloween I was (or will be)
—My favorite Halloween costume is
—I can draw a jack-o'-lantern face

As the children arrive, give each of them a marker and ask them to respond on the newsprint in graffiti-like fashion. When all are present, take a couple of minutes to discuss some of these special Halloween memories.

Sing a Halloween Song (5 to 10 minutes)

Before class time ask one or two of the children to prepare to teach a Halloween song to the class. Most children will know several that they have learned in school.

Or, you might teach the class "Halloween Is Coming," by Steve Edwards.

Halloween is Coming

by Steve Edwards

Ghosts & goblins in the air, Halloween is coming.
It will give us all a scare, Halloween is coming.
Witches flying in the sky, Hide your head as they pass by.
Skeletons and monsters cry. Halloween is coming.

©1983 by Faith Designs. Used by permission.

All Saints' Day (5 minutes)

Briefly relate to the children the origin of Halloween. A long time ago a day was set aside (November 1) to honor all the heroes of the church—people who had done great things for Jesus and all of God's children. These people were called saints, and the day was called All Saints' Day. (In Britain it was called All Hallows' Day.) The night before was Hallows' Eve (or Halloween). People believed it was

116

then that witches, devils, and goblins came out to cause trouble for the saints. That is how Halloween began. But the focus was not on the ghosts and goblins; it was on the saints. So now we are going to learn some things about the saints and how we might be saints ourselves.

Developing Activities

To introduce the stories of two saints, hold up the red heart and the green shamrock. Ask the children to name the persons associated with the heart and shamrock. They will probably to able to mention Saints Valentine and Patrick.

Then ask the children, "What do you think it was about these people that made other people call them saints? What is a saint?" Suggest that maybe the children will be able to list qualities of saints after they hear stories of the saints' lives.

Tell the following story:

The Story of Saint Valentine

Valentine was a Roman priest who lived over seventeen hundred years ago during a time when many Christians in Rome were being persecuted. Because Valentine helped these Christians, he was put in prison and condemned to die. Even while in prison, Valentine helped people. He became friends with the jailkeeper's blind daughter, and through prayer he helped her to regain her sight. The story is told that, on the night before he was executed, Valentine wrote a farewell message to the jailkeeper's daughter saying that he would remember her for all eternity. He signed the message "From Your Valentine."

February 14th is Saint Valentine's Day. Every year we give special messages to people to let them know that we care for them, much in the same way Saint Valentine cared for people.

As a group, list on chalkboard or newsprint some qualities of a saint as shown by Valentine. (He helped people in need, he cared for people who hurt him, he did miracles through prayer, he died for his faith.)

Then tell the following story:

The Story of Saint Patrick

Patrick was a missionary to Ireland over fifteen hundred years ago. At this time Ireland was ruled by fierce warriors with iron swords and wooden shields. When Patrick was a boy in Britain, his home was raided by Irish warriors. He was carried away to Ireland and became a slave. Patrick was very lonely as a slave, but he found comfort by praying to the Christian God many times a day. After six years he escaped and through much peril made his way back home to Britain. A few years later the British church wanted to send missionaries to Ireland. Although Patrick had many reasons to hate the Irish people, he volunteered. He had forgiven them for all the terrible things they had done to him, and he spent the rest of his life in Ireland building churches and helping people become Christians. Today, on Saint Patrick's Day, all Irish Christians remember Patrick's forgiveness and celebrate the wonderful things his mission accomplished.

St. Patrick showed many saintly qualities. Ask the children to add them to their list of saintly qualities. Some of these are: He forgave people who hurt him, he gave up his home and friends to help strangers, he built new churches.

Sing a Song (10 to 15 minutes)

On newsprint put the words of the song "I Sing a Song of the Saints of God." Teach it to the children, making sure they understand all of the words.

Give one child a colored marker. With the help of the class ask the child to circle all the different kinds of people mentioned in the song (doctor, queen, soldier, priest, etc.). Give a second child a different colored marker. Ask this

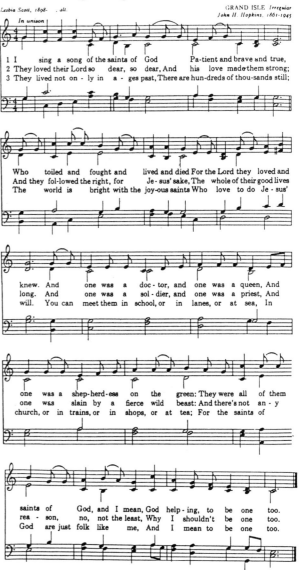

I Sing a Song of the Saints of God

117

child to circle qualities of the saints mentioned in the song (patient, brave, strong, good, etc.). A third child could circle all the places saints can be found (school, church, shops, etc.).

After studying the song in this way, sing it one more time with as much enthusiasm as possible.

What the Bible Says (5 to 10 minutes)

Help the children read 2 Corinthians 5:16-21 (TEV). Discuss how Valentine and Patrick changed enemies into friends. If we are to become saints, we too must help change enemies into friends. This may be hard to do, but verse 17 gives a hint about how it can be done.

Learning Centers (20 to 30 minutes)

Let the children choose one or more of the following activities, depending on time and interests.

Create a drama: A group of children may want to put together a short play based on the story of Saint Valentine or Saint Patrick. Provide props and costumes that may be helpful.

Write a story: Some may like to write a story about how an enemy at school was changed into a friend. Provide writing paper and perhaps a typewriter.

Interview a saint: Two or three children may wish to create a tape of an interview with Valentine and Patrick, or a modern-day saint. Provide a cassette recorder and blank tape.

Draw a valentine: Some may choose to create a valentine to give to a saint in your church, telling why that person is a saint. Provide necessary materials. (You may need to give suggestions.) If it is not the valentine season, this activity might be even more interesting.

Make a poster: Some may make a poster showing with pictures and/or words things children can do today to be saint-like.

Write a prayer/poem/song: Some may write a prayer, poem, or song thanking God for the saints or seeking God's help to be saint-like.

Closing Activities

Make a Shield (10 to 15 minutes)

Provide materials for each child to begin to reproduce the "All Saints Shield" on posterboard, newsprint, or con-

struction paper. The shield is the symbol for all saints. You may need to plan carefully about how you will imitate gold, since gold paint is expensive. Gold gift wrap or gold glitter may be easier to get in your situation. Silver can be represented by aluminum foil. The crown is gold and refers to sanctity. The scrolls are also gold and the words of the chant of the redeemed are in red on the scrolls. The left

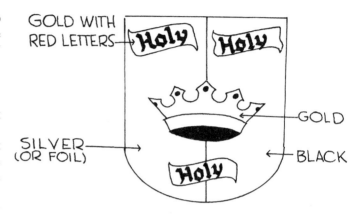

All Saints' Shield

half of the shield is silver, representing the brightness of the heavenly life, while the right half is black, signifying the trials of the earthly life. You might prepare a completed sample for the children to see (see the illustration above).

Final Sharing (5 to 10 minutes)

Allow brief sharing of some of the center activities done earlier. There will probably not be time for everyone to share.

Mention that Paul said the Christians in Rome were "called to be saints" (Romans 1:7 RSV). We too are called to be saints today. Close with a prayer written by one of the children, thanking God for the saints and seeking help to be saint-like.

> **Bible Used in This Session**: 2 Corinthians 5:16-21; Romans 1:7

Session 2

A Saint the Children Love

Purpose

- To introduce the children to the historical Saint Nicholas and show how the modern Santa Claus is like him.
- To inspire the children to model a lifestyle of selfless giving evident in the life of Saint Nicholas.

Background for Leader(s)

The legends about the life and deeds of Saint Nicholas are far too numerous to deal with in one session. They range from delightful stories of his selfless generosity and sense of justice to superhuman stories of apparitions, healings, and raising people from the dead. He has been the patron saint of children, seafaring men, marriageable young women, merchants, the falsely accused, endangered travelers, farmers, and even pawnbrokers.

Santa Claus, as we know him, was a creation of nineteenth-century New York and three creative artists. Yet in him are the basic qualities of Saint Nicholas which have been honored down through the years, namely, assurance, trust, piety, kindness, and selflessness. For an easy-to-read account of how Saint Nicholas became Santa Claus, find *Saint Nicholas Life and Legend*, by Martin Ebon (New York: Harper & Row, Publishers, Inc., 1975). This book contains many wonderful photos and illustrations which you and the children will enjoy.

Beginning Activities

Sing a Song (10 minutes)

Sing "I Sing a Song of the Saints of God" from Session 1 if you taught it then. If not, begin to teach it now. Also, briefly explain to the children that saints are the heroes of the church—people who have done great things for Jesus and all of God's children.

Saint Nicholas and Santa Claus (5 to 10 minutes)

Introduce Saint Nicholas with words like these:

About seventeen hundred years ago there lived a priest named Nicholas. He was born in Turkey and later became a famous bishop in the city of Myra. A bishop was a high-ranking minister in the church. (You might want to show the map found on page 120 and point out where Nicholas lived.) Nicholas was a kind,

selfless, giving man all of his life. He became famous throughout the entire world for helping people in need.

Today we are all familiar with Santa Claus, a white-bearded, jolly man in a red suit who is said to come down chimneys at Christmastime to leave presents for boys and girls. "Santa" is another word for "saint" and "Claus" is a short form of "Nicholas." Saint Nicholas and Santa Claus are the same person, but Saint Nicholas lived in Turkey, not the North Pole. He rode a white horse, not a sleigh drawn by reindeer, and he was tall and thin, not short and fat. Of course Nicholas does not still live today, but it is good for us to remember him as the kind, generous man he was.

Developing Activities

There are many stories about the life of Saint Nicholas. Two of these are presented here. Choose one of them and some of the related activities which follow them. If you have more than one adult leader, you may divide the group and have two different stories being told at the same time.

A Saint for Justice (15 to 20 minutes)

One day as Saint Nicholas was walking on the streets of Myra, he saw a group of men and women who were crying. There was a wicked official in Myra who was willing to execute innocent people if their enemies would bribe him. The weeping men and women told Nicholas that this wicked official had condemned three innocent men to death, who were about to be beheaded in the center of town. Other townspeople told Nicholas this was true, so he ran angrily to the place of execution. He stopped the hand of the executioner and took away his sword just before it came down on the first man. Nicholas untied the ropes of the victims and set them free. When the wicked official saw what was happening, he started to run away. Nicholas stopped him and threatened to tell the emperor about this disgraceful act. The official became frightened. On his knees he confessed his injustice, and Nicholas forgave him.

For Discussion

a. What injustice had the wicked official committed?
b. Did Saint Nicholas do the right thing?
c. Would you have forgiven the official?

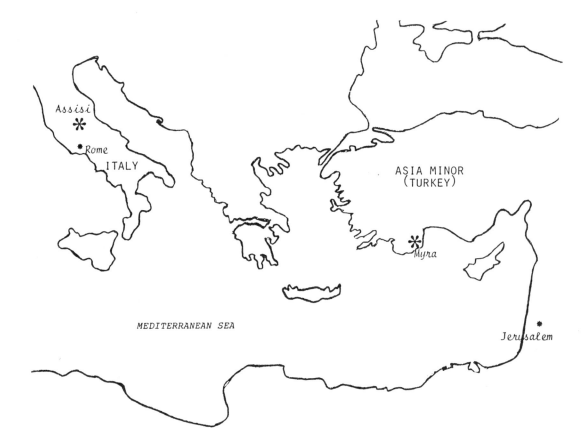

Assisi
*
* Rome
ITALY

ASIA MINOR
(TURKEY)

*
Myra

*
Jerusalem

MEDITERRANEAN SEA

To Do

a. With the entire group act out the story. The cast will include Saint Nicholas, the wicked official, the executioner, the three victims, the weeping relatives, and the townspeople. This could be a good melodrama with the group calling out "Boo!" and "Yea!" at appropriate times.

b. Make a justice collage. Ask the class to cut pictures of injustice out of magazines and glue them to posterboard or newsprint to make one large collage. Discuss how each picture depicts injustice in today's world and how perhaps this injustice could be eliminated.

A Generous Saint (15 to 20 minutes)

Even as a young man, before he became bishop of Myra, Nicholas was a kind and generous person. One time he heard that a sad father was going to have to sell one of his teenage daughters in order to provide for the other two. It seems the father did not have enough money to care for his daughters. Nicholas secretly tied a large sum of money in a handkerchief and, after dark, threw it through an open window of the sad father's house for her dowry. (A dowry was a sum of money which each young woman had to have before she could get married.) Thus the first daughter was saved. Soon, however, the family was in trouble again, and it looked as though the second daughter would have to be sold. Nicholas repeated the good deed and saved the second daughter. When the third daughter was in a similar danger, the father caught Nicholas throwing the money through the window. He thanked him for saving his family, for each of the three girls used the money as her dowry. Embarrassed,

Nicholas asked the father not to tell anyone what he had done. It was not until Nicholas died that the father told everyone about the generous deed of the young saint.

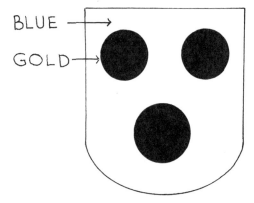

BLUE ➞

GOLD ➞

Shield of Saint Nicholas

For Discussion

a. If you did something like this, would you want it to be kept secret?

b. How is this story about Saint Nicholas similar to stories about Santa Claus?

To Do

a. Make a shield of Saint Nicholas (see the illustration). Provide materials for each child to reproduce the symbol on posterboard or newsprint. The three gold balls represent the bags of money Nicholas used to save the three girls. The background is blue.

Also provide materials to complete the shields begun in Session 1.

b. Create a slide show or filmstrip telling the story. This could be a small-group activity. Kodak Ektagraphic write-on slides can be used to draw pictures of the story. Or old filmstrips can be stripped by soaking them in bleach. The children can then draw on the slides or filmstrips with felt-tipped markers. Use the ''Filmstrip Making Guide'' diagram shown here to determine where each frame should be. Leave about 2 inches (5.1 cm) before the first frame.

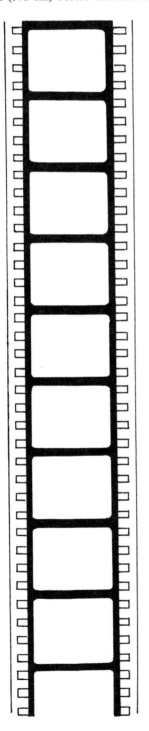

Closing Activities

What the Bible Says (5 to 10 minutes)

Matthew 2:1-12. The generosity of Saint Nicholas has been related to the story of the wise men bringing gifts to the infant Jesus. The combination of this biblical story with the legends of Saint Nicholas has developed into the modern practice of gift giving at Christmas and the beautiful stories of Santa Claus, the embodiment of selfless giving.

Gift Giving (5 to 10 minutes)

Put the name of each child who is present in the group today on a separate piece of paper. Fold the papers with the names inside. Let each child select a slip of paper, making sure not to keep her or his own name. Suggest that ''One way we can give gifts is to draw or write something we might like to give the person whose name we have.'' Help the children understand they are not limited to drawing things they can touch, like toys or books. Suggest that they can give a gift-wish for good health, good marks at school, friendship, and so on.

Just before the children hand the ''gifts'' to one another, pause to give thanks in prayer for one another and for the help the group and church give them as they try to be saints.

Bible Used in This Session: Matthew 2:1-12.

Session 3

A Saint of All Living Things

Purpose

- To introduce the children to Saint Francis, his kindness to animals, and his great reverence for nature, through one of his poems.
- To discover the human responsibility towards God's creation.
- To worship God as revealed in creation.

Background for Leader(s)

It was a personal joy for me to research the life and writings of Saint Francis of Assisi in preparation for this session. He can surely be an inspiration for all Christian people. Francis was deeply devoted to the cross of Christ, had a great reverence for nature, was compassionate to animals as well as to humans, and carried self-denial to its limits. The Franciscan order, founded by Saint Francis, is based on obedience, poverty, and chastity. Franciscan brothers have dedicated themselves to this lifestyle for almost eight hundred years, and, although the ways they express these qualities are not requirements for the Christian faith, one must admire the commitment to Christ and the church which the brothers exhibit in their vows.

Saint Francis expressed much of his devotion in poetry and music. He wrote ''All Creatures of Our God and King'' near the end of his life when his health was gone and his sight fading. Yet he could still appreciate the beauty of the creation and sing praises to God. It is his reverence for nature and kindness to animals that children will most appreciate about Saint Francis. It is important that children be led to express their own love for nature and accept our human responsibility of caring for all creation. Therefore the closing worship experience is important to this session. Be careful to develop an atmosphere and attitude for worship to happen.

''The Prayer of Saint Francis'' is probably one of his best known writings. Although the children do not deal with it in this session, it is appropriate for the leader(s) to be reminded of his words in preparation for the session.

Lord, make me an instrument of thy peace.
Where there is hatred, let me sow love;
where there is injury, pardon;
where there is discord, union;
where there is doubt, faith;
where there is despair, hope;

where there is darkness, light;
and where there is sadness, joy.
Divine Master, grant that I may not so much seek
to be consoled as to console;
to be understood as to understand;
to be loved as to love;
for it is in giving that we receive,
it is in pardoning that we are pardoned,
and it is in dying that we are born to eternal life.

—Saint Francis of Assisi

In preparation for this session gather these items: pencils, two or three pipe cleaners per child, scissors, cotton balls, colored chalk, markers, colored pencils, crayons, tempera paints, construction paper, glue, and aluminum foil.

Beginning Activities

Hidden Word Puzzle (5 to 10 minutes)

As children arrive, give them a copy of the hidden word puzzle which appears on page 123.

If you have no way to make individual copies, post the puzzle on a bulletin board and give the children pencils and paper. When they see a word, they can put it on their paper forward or backward or on a slant—just as they see it in the puzzle. The words in this puzzle are taken from ''The Canticle of Brother Sun'' by Saint Francis and will begin to introduce the children to his reverence for nature.

Animal Creations (10 minutes)

Ask each child to create some kind of animal out of two or three pipe cleaners. If you have cotton balls, glue, and colored paper, add them to the supply of pipe cleaners. A variety of interesting shapes can be made by bending and twisting pipe cleaners together. They can be easily cut with an old pair of scissors if shorter pieces are desired. The animals may be running, leaping, walking, or lying down. You may want to prepare a couple of samples prior to class time to give the children an idea of what can be done. Find an appropriate place to display these wonderful creations.

Saint Francis of Assisi (5 to 10 minutes)

Show the photo of Saint Francis as you relate some of the following information about him to the children:

Hidden Word Puzzle

Directions: The following words are hidden in this puzzle. They are written across, up and down, and diagonally, and may be forwards or backwards. Circle the words you can find . . .

AIR	DAY	SISTER MOTHER
BROTHER FIRE	FLOWERS	EARTH
BROTHER SUN	FRUITS	SISTER MOON
BROTHER WIND	HERBS	SISTER WATER
CLOUDS	LIGHT	STARS
		WEATHER

```
H  B  R  O  T  H  E  R  S  U  N  P  I  F  T  H  E
A  T  X  O  V  B  S  T  E  N  O  P  Q  U  B  R  T
P  H  R  B  T  H  O  R  E  A  O  N  M  W  R  O  O
I  G  D  A  O  P  U  X  T  R  M  E  C  Z  O  T  H
S  I  S  T  E  R  W  A  T  E  R  Y  O  U  T  E  A
F  L  A  S  T  R  E  H  T  A  E  W  N  O  H  C  H
Y  E  C  H  O  U  E  R  P  H  T  X  Y  Z  E  S  W
S  I  C  F  N  G  A  H  N  E  S  W  S  O  R  N  G
A  L  L  R  C  R  E  T  A  I  T  U  A  F  R  E
S  O  F  O  O  U  O  U  R  O  S  G  T  O  I  D  A
N  D  K  W  I  U  I  N  G  L  M  S  I  F  R  T  U
P  Y  O  E  U  R  D  T  V  O  I  R  C  E  E  A  N
W  H  I  R  T  H  U  S  S  S  Y  I  E  N  G  A  L
L  E  E  S  L  U  I  A  O  P  A  R  A  T  I  S  E
B  R  O  T  H  E  R  W  I  N  D  H  I  M  S  O  P
R  B  A  I  S  E  I  H  I  M  T  H  E  C  A  I  N
T  S  I  C  L  E  A  O  F  Z  E  R  Q  U  B  X  S
```

Answers:

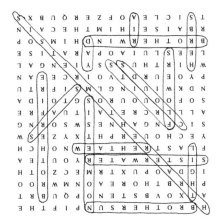

123

About eight hundred years ago Saint Francis lived in the Italian city of Assisi (see map on page 120). His father was a wealthy merchant, so in his childhood Francis had all he ever needed or wanted. But as an adult he took a vow of poverty, believing that was the best way he could serve Christ and the church. Others who believed as Francis did began to look to him as their leader. They formed a group called the Franciscan order, and that group still exists today. At one time the members were called "monks" and "friars." Today they usually refer to themselves as "brothers."

Francis is also well known for his kindness to animals and his love for all nature. Often he would spend time alone with animals, talking to them, feeding them, and helping them when they were hurt. He wrote poetry and songs that praised God for the wonderful things in nature. In a poem called "The Canticle of Brother Sun" Francis calls the sun "brother," the moon "sister," and the earth "sister mother." He loved God's creation as if it were his own family. Saint Francis has helped us all to learn how we can be closer to God when we appreciate God's creation.

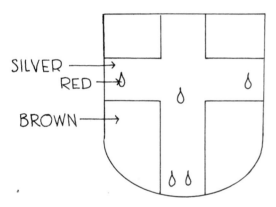

Shield of Saint Francis

Developing Activities

What the Bible Says (10 to 15 minutes)

Genesis 1:26-31. Saint Francis' kindness to animals and his love for nature were based on Bible passages such as this one. Remind the children of the creation story and point out our responsibility for taking care of what God has made.

Psalm 8:1-9. This song may well have inspired Saint Francis to write his poems and songs about nature. Ask the children for specific ways they see God in the world (flowers, butterflies, people). This passage also points out our responsibility for God's creation.

A Mural of a Hymn (20 to 30 minutes)

The original words of "All Creatures of Our God and King" were taken from Saint Francis' poem. Sing it with the children.

Call attention to the different parts of creation mentioned. Also ask such things as "Who is the king mentioned?" Talk also about the old-fashioned language—"ye, thou," "givest," and "man" (which includes women and children)—and the reverse wording, such as "Let them his glory show." By pointing out some of these features, the song becomes more meaningful to the children.

Then, as a group, create a mural that depicts the words. A mural is a group of pictures on a large sheet of paper arranged to express a single idea. In this case that idea is "all creation praising God." A mural is best done by hanging the paper on the wall before the pictures are drawn. The children can sketch their ideas on separate sheets of paper and transfer them to the mural paper. A fun medium to use is colored chalk, but you could also use colored pencils, markers, crayons, or tempera paints. You might want to tape on your pipe-cleaner animals, too.

Give a title to your mural, and be sure everyone contributes to the finished product.

Learning Centers (20 to 30 minutes)

This is an alternate activity. Let the children choose one or more of the following activities, depending on time and interest.

Make pipe-cleaner figures: Some may like to make more animals with pipe cleaners. Ask them to create all the figures in the creation story (Genesis 1). Colored construction paper can be cut and glued to the figures to make them more realistic. Provide pipe cleaners, scissors, glue, and construction paper.

Origami: Several interesting animals can be made using the art of folding paper. Perhaps you know someone who can do this with the children. This is a rather precise art, however, and requires patience. There are several good books with detailed instructions. One is *Origami, The Art of Paperfolding*, by Robert Harbin (New York: Barnes & Noble Books, 1982). Secure this or another book on Origami from your local library.

Write a poem: *Haiku* is a simple form of poetry that children do well. It consists of only three lines. The first line must have five syllables; the second seven; and the third, five syllables again. There is no need to be concerned with rhyme. Ask the children to write *Haiku* poems about taking care of God's Creation.

Example: God made the whole world.
    We must be kind to God's world.
    Take care of all things.

These poems could be put on newsprint or construction paper and hung on the wall.

Create a shield: Provide materials for the children to reproduce the shield of Saint Francis. It is said that he bore the marks of the Lord's suffering and death on his hands, feet, and side for two years before his death. The background is brown, the cross silver (use foil to represent silver). The marks are red.

Also provide for completing any shields which may not have been finished in Session 1 of this unit.

Closing Activities

Final Sharing (5 minutes)

If the learning centers were used, take a couple of minutes to share some of the things the children did and make some application of them to the session purposes. Ask such questions as: "What was it about Francis that would cause people to name him as a saint?" "How do you feel when you sing the hymn he wrote?"

If the class worked on the mural together, take a few moments for responses to the project.

Closing Worship (10 minutes)

Read Psalm 8 as a choral reading. . . . Write verse 1a (the same as verse 9) on the chalkboard or newsprint. Have the whole class read that verse. One child then reads verses 1b and 2. Another child reads verses 3 and 4. A third child reads verses 5 through 8. Finally, the class repeats verse 9.

Sing "All Creatures of Our God and King."

Ask each child to name one specific thing he or she can do to take care of God's creation.

Close with prayer. Have the children form a circle and ask each child to thank God for one specific thing in nature.

Bible Used in This Session: Genesis 1; Psalm 8

Session 4

You Can Be a Saint

Purpose

- To review learnings from the first three sessions of this unit.
- To acquaint children with Marcella, a woman who was a saint of the early church.
- To help children see how their response to Jesus can make them a saint, too.

Background for Leader(s)

Two things need to happen in this session. The unit on "The Saints of God" needs to be brought to a close. Unfinished projects should be completed; but unanswered questions can lead to future discovery and thought. The children are beginning to learn what they can do to become saints of God.

The beginning activities are designed to meet the first objective. Make sure the children realize that this is the last opportunity to complete projects or repeat activities. Allow plenty of time for this work. The children may work individually, in pairs, or with small groups. The leader's role is primarily one of assistance and encouragement.

The major input for this session comes from Romans 12:9-21. The principles found here are being called "The Acts of the Saints" and can be put in two groups. In verses 9-13 Paul identifies ten rules for saintly living.

1. Love must be completely sincere.
2. Hate what is evil, hold to what is good.
3. Be affectionate with one another.
4. Respect each other, eagerly.
5. Be zealous, not sluggish.
6. Act enthusiastically, on fire for Christ.
7. Serve the Lord.
8. Rejoice in hope.
9. Be patient with troubles.
10. Abide in prayer.

Verses 14-21 point out seven relational principles.

1. Pray for those who persecute you.
2. Empathize with one another.
3. Live in harmony with each other.
4. Avoid pride in self.
5. Act for the good of all.
6. Live at peace with all people.
7. Do not seek revenge.

Paul's words are simple and to the point. Anyone who follows these guidelines will certainly be considered a saint of God. But how can children understand these things and follow them? Any learning activities you can lead to help the children explore these Christlike principles will be beneficial. The boys and girls will most likely learn how to be saints by observing saints in action. The *greatest* challenge for you as a leader of children is not to develop wonderful teaching techniques, although these are important, but to *be* a saint—to act out the ten rules for saintly living daily, and to relate to all people (students, family, friends, and even strangers) according to Paul's seven relational principles. Our children imitate what they see. If we act as saints of God, they too will develop saint-like characteristics.

A story of Marcella, who died in A.D. 410, is included as another example of one whose life exemplified Paul's guidelines.

In preparation for this session gather these materials: finger paint (or starch and poster paint, which can be substituted for commercially prepared finger paint); glossy paper; aprons; newspapers to protect tabletops.

Beginning Activities

Review of Unit (20 to 25 minutes)

As the children arrive, help them choose to do one or more of the following activities. Some may enjoy repeating an activity they liked earlier in the unit. Others may want to complete something they have already begun. This is important work to enable closure of the unit.

a. *Shields of the saints*: Provide materials for the children to draw the shields of Saint Nicholas and Saint Francis, and the All Saints' Shield. *Saints, Signs and Symbols*, by W. Ellwood Post (Wilton, Conn.: Morehouse-Barlow Co., Inc. 1974) contains the symbols of many other saints which the children may like to copy.

b. *Sing and respond to a song*: Some may like to sing "I Sing a Song of the Saints of God" and "All Creatures of Our God and King." You could put these on a cassette tape so the children can easily sing along. They may also like to add to the mural from Session 3 or create a new mural for "I Sing a Song of the Saints of God."

c. *Hidden word puzzle*: Children who did not do the puzzle in Session 3 may wish to do it now. Other children may like to create a hidden word puzzle with words related to Saint Nicholas or words about being a saint.

d. *Slide show or filmstrip*: If a slide show or filmstrip was created during Session 2 some children may want to review it and possibly do a new one at this time.

e. *Animal figures*: The pipe-cleaner or origami figures from Session 3 could be repeated by interested children.

Before moving on, take a minute to remind the entire class of the activities related to Saint Francis and Saint Nicholas and also the stories of Saint Patrick and Saint Valentine.

Developing Activities

What the Bible Says (10 to 15 minutes)

Remind the children that Saint Paul has said that we are all "called to be saints" (Romans 1:7). We are going to study some other words of Paul to help us know how you and I can be saints today.

Romans 12:9-21. Read this passage one verse at a time. After reading each verse, list on chalkboard or newsprint the "Acts of the Saints" as follows:

verse 9 . . . hate evil
             do good

verse 10 . . . love each other
             respect each other

verse 11 . . . work hard
             serve God

verse 12 . . . be joyful
             be patient
             always pray

verse 13 . . . share with others
             welcome strangers

verse 14 . . . forgive your enemies

verse 15 . . . feel for others

verse 16 . . . care for all people
             be humble

verse 17 . . . repay evil with good

verse 18 . . . live in peace

verse 19 . . . never seek revenge

verse 20 . . . help your enemies

verse 21 . . . conquer evil with good

Finger Painting (10 to 15 minutes)

In response to the Scripture study, ask each child to create a finger painting about the acts of the saints. Finger painting is best done as abstract art. Remind the children that the way they use color can show ideas and feelings as well as shapes and lines can. "Evil" does not need to be shown in black or dark tones. (Dark-haired or dark-skinned people sometimes resent evil being depicted as black or dark.) Sometimes evil is shown by explosive use of color or by the absence of color. Likewise, "good" does not have to be seen in white or light colors.

Placement on the paper should indicate how their ideas interact with each other.

Don't be afraid of this project. The children will enjoy it and will create some insightful paintings. They may need some encouragement, however, as well as supervision. Each child will need a smock of some kind to protect clothing, and damp cloths or sponges need to be available to clean hands and spills. Special finger-painting paper works best (normal paper absorbs too much paint and does not dry well), but a glossy shelf paper will also work well. Good finger paints can be purchased from your local art supply store or can be made by mixing powdered tempera paints with liquid starch.

Gathering Women for God (10 minutes)

After they have cleaned up from the finger painting, invite the children to listen to another story of a saint from long ago. Although most of the people you have talked about as saints have been men, women were also brave followers of Jesus.

Tell the story of Marcella, "Gathering Women for God."

Gathering Women for God

When the church was just beginning, life was very different for women from what it is now. Young women were expected to get married and live under the protection of their husbands. They were not free to choose their work or to do whatever they wanted. Usually they were not even taught to read and write.

Rich people lived mainly for parties, with fancy food and dress, and often had slaves.

It might have been just that way for Marcella, too. She married a rich man, but when he died after only seven months, she changed her life.

She began to study the Bible and opened her home to the great Bible teacher and translator, Jerome. Other women came to Marcella's home to learn about the Bible from Jerome while he stayed in Rome at Marcella's home for three years. Often she took care of Christian travelers while they were hiding from enemies or on their way to preach the gospel.

She decided that she did not need fancy clothes and the kind of life that went with being rich. Instead she wore a plain brown dress and was kind to poor and sick people. Other rich women saw what she was doing, and they joined her in a group. In this way she began one of the first convents or centers for Christian women where they stayed to pray, study the Bible, and help the poor.

When enemies came through Rome, many Christians were wounded and went to Marcella's religious center for help. They were followed there by the soldiers. The soldiers thought Marcella had money hidden somewhere, but in reality she had spent it on keeping the convent open to serve the poor. The soldiers beat Marcella, yet she begged them to spare the lives of the other women. At the time she was eighty-five years old. In a few days, she died from that torture. It was the year A.D. 410. Later, she was named a saint of the church.[1]

After the story, briefly refer to the list of saintly qualities you have listed on chalkboard or newsprint from Romans 12. Ask the children to tell which of the ''Acts of the Saints'' are shown in Marcella's life.

A Modern-Day Saint (5 to 10 minutes)

Invite an adult in your congregation to come and talk with the children. This should be someone who is highly devoted to God and could share with the class how he or she has followed and is following Jesus. In preparation for this time give your guest the above Bible study and suggest it be a guide.

If you are unable to invite a guest to the class you may want to share a story about some saintly person in modern times, such as Martin Luther King, Jr., Mother Teresa of Calcutta, Archbishop Romero, or some other appropriate person.

The children may already realize that there are people in modern times who exhibit the qualities of sainthood that have been identified in each session of this unit. Ask them to call out names of people whom they would include in a list of saints today. Put these names on newsprint or chalkboard. If there is time, ask the children to explain their nominations. Such a process may help them distinguish between those who are merely popular and those who serve God.

Closing Activities

Personal Symbols (10 to 15 minutes)

Help each child create a shield with a personal symbol

[1] Edith Deen, *Great Women of the Christian Faith* (New York: Harper & Row, Publishers, Inc., 1959), pp. 17-21.

that describes a saint-like characteristic he or she possesses. Joy could be represented by a smiling face. A heart could represent love. A hand could mean you welcome strangers. A hammer could mean that you work hard. Praying hands could represent prayerfulness. A dove could stand for peace, or some other animal could show your love for creation. Christian symbols such as the cross, a fish, or a Bible could also be used. Help each child to identify his or her saint-like qualities and symbolize them in a personal shield. You may create a symbol for yourself also.

A Saintly Promise (5 to 10 minutes)

Display on newsprint or posterboard a statement like the following one:

I want to be a saint of God, so I promise to do my best to live like a saint of God by:

—forgiving my enemies
—helping people in need
—working for justice
—giving selflessly to others
—taking care of God's creation
—working hard
—serving God
—praying always
—doing good
—loving all people
    and
—living like Jesus

Ask the children who want to make this promise to post their shields around the newsprint and to sign their names at the bottom of the ''Saintly Promise.''

Close by singing ''I Sing a Song of the Saints of God.''

Bible Used in This Session: Romans 12:9-21